"Are your parents divorced? This book is for you. Kristine Steakley writes from experience—her own and others'. She weaves a mosaic of hope out of the threads of Scripture, research, literature, movies and real-life stories."

LEITH ANDERSON, president, National Association of Evangelicals, and pastor, Wooddale Church, Eden Prairie, Minnesota

"In a culture where a majority of families have been torn by divorce, Kristine has filled these pages with healing and hope straight from God's Word. No matter what age you are, if you have experienced the raw pain of your parents' divorce, these words can bring revelation and cut through the myriad emotions and thoughts you experience. Parents, please read to understand how absolutely vital it is for you to help your children through one of the most difficult seasons of their life."

RON LUCE, president and founder, Teen Mania Ministries

"A tender exploration of the hardships and comforts a growing child of divorce finds in a life of faith. Steakley's story will be familiar to anyone who, despite the broken family dreams of the past, has sought to find wholeness in the Christian faith."

ELIZABETH MARQUARDT, author of *Between Two Worlds: The Inner Lives of Children of Divorce*

"Kristine Steakley sensitively addresses the wounds that many children of divorce bear so bravely. By pointing them to the One who binds up the broken-hearted, she does more than many books written on the subject of divorce: she not only addresses the issues, but offers real hope for healing."

CHUCK COLSON, founder, Prison Fellowship

"*Child of Divorce, Child of God* is a must-read for every young-adult child of divorce as well as adults whose parents divorced years ago. Kristine expertly weaves the Word of God throughout the entire book. Her personal stories and insights will captivate every reader and bring them to a deep understanding of God's call for them. Her words bring hope and comfort and let the reader know that they are not alone in their quest to find healing for the wounds of today and from the scars of yesterday."

LINDA RANSON JACOBS, executive director, DivorceCare for Kids

CHILD OF DIVORCE, CHILD OF GOD

A Journey of Hope and Healing

Kristine Steakley

IVP Books

An imprint of InterVarsity Press
Downers Grove, Illinois

InterVarsity Press
P.O. Box 1400, Downers Grove, IL 60515-1426
World Wide Web: www.ivpress.com
E-mail: email@ivpress.com

InterVarsity Press® is the book-publishing division of InterVarsity Christian Fellowship/USA®, a student
movement active on campus at hundreds of universities, colleges and schools of nursing in the United
States of America, and a member movement of the International Fellowship of Evangelical Students.
For information about local and regional activities, write Public Relations Dept., InterVarsity Christian
Fellowship/USA, 6400 Schroeder Rd., P.O. Box 7895, Madison, WI 53707-7895, or visit the IVCF website
at <www.intervarsity.org>.

While all the stories in this book are true, some names and identifying details have been changed to
protect the privacy of the people involved.

Design: Cindy Kiple
Images: father and daughter: iStockphoto
      hand holding frame: Mel Curtis/Getty Images

ISBN 978-0-8308-3471-6

Typeset by The Livingstone Corporation (www.LivingstoneCorp.com).

Printed in the United States of America ∞

Library of Congress Cataloging-in-Publication Data

Steakley, Kristine, 1970-
  Child of divorce, child of God: a journey of hope and healing /
  Kristine Steakley.
      p. cm.
  Includes bibliographical references.
  ISBN 978-0-8308-3471-6 (pbk.: alk. paper)
  1. Divorce—Religious aspects—Christianity. 2. Children of
  divorced parents—Religious life. I. Title.
  BT707.S734 2008
  248.8'46—dc22

                                                              2008017359

P 18 17 16 15 14 13 12 11 10 9 8 7 6 5 4 3 2

Y 23 22 21 20 19 18 17 16 15 14 13 12 11 10 09

Contents

Introduction

Three-year-old Krissy stands at the window, her mom by her side. Outside, Krissy's dad drives away in his car while Krissy and Mom wave goodbye. It sounds like a common enough memory—and it would be, except that it is the only memory Krissy will ever have of her mom and dad together.

More than thirty years later, that memory still makes my heart weep for the child I was. That was me, waving goodbye to Daddy. I cannot tell you whether this particular memory was of him leaving for work on an ordinary day or driving away for the very last time, but the irony that this is my only early memory of my dad—and my only memory of my mom and dad together—is not lost on me. Most of my memories begin during the time Mom and I were living in the first-floor apartment of a house in her hometown.

My mom and dad married young. He had just graduated from college; she left school after two years to marry him. I was born less than a year later, and only three years after that, their marriage was over. I was too young to remember much about that time, but my uncle recently sent me a cassette tape of audio recordings, mostly of me and my grandparents, from the year that my mom and dad divorced. At the beginning of the tape, I am prattling on about Mommy and Daddy and our new house and the puppy I was sure they would get me. By the end of the tape, I am visiting Daddy in his new apartment in another state.

When I was five, my mom married my stepfather. They just celebrated their thirty-second wedding anniversary, and from their marriage I have two brothers who have both grown into fine men. My story is largely a happy one, but as you'll read in these pages, it was not without difficulty. My relationship with my dad has been particularly difficult. When I was seventeen years old, my dad cut off all contact with me for the next eight years. There was no fight, no explanation; he simply disappeared from my life. And it was not as if he took off for Tibet or some remote Pacific island and no one heard from him for eight years. My grandparents, my uncle and other relatives all spoke to him regularly, visited with him, heard from him. I alone, it seemed, had been abandoned.

Recently I was chatting with a casual acquaintance about growing up in a family with divorce. Her husband's parents are divorced, and yet (oddly, to my mind) they are still very intertwined in each other's lives. The complexities of families—the unique combinations of passions, personalities, values, intellects and a dozen other factors that somehow knit us together into clans as distinct as handmade afghans—defy convention or the expectations or experiences of others. I could no more relate to the separate-involved-together-apart kind of life of this other family than I could envision living marooned on an island of zebras. Both would be unfathomably difficult to navigate or reconcile. We had a good long chat, and I recommended several books for her and her husband.

Then I said, as innocently as pre-apple Eve, "I can't ever remember my mom and dad being in the same room together." I might as well have grown a second head for the astonished look she gave me. It had not seemed an odd thing to say, just a simple statement of truth.

"Wow, their divorce must have been really acrimonious," she said.

"No, I don't think it was," I responded. "But afterward, they never really had a need to be in the same place." It was simple enough. My mom and I no longer lived in the same town as my dad. When I visited him, my grandparents—who were self-employed and had more flexibility in their schedule—would pick me up at my mom's and bring me back a few days later. After I finished first grade, my mom, my new stepfather and I moved to another state, and from then on I traveled alone by airplane between my two families.

To be honest, I am not sure how I would handle a collision of those two worlds. My friend Karen used to hate the idea of casseroles, with their bits of peas and chicken and potatoes and sauce all mixing together with total abandon. I have always liked casseroles, but the idea of my mom and my dad in the same room is just too weird—like eating butterscotch pudding and scalloped potatoes together. Sure, they are both creamy and tasty and good enough on their own, but they aren't meant to go together.

Of course, my mom and dad were together at one point. I have pictures of the two of them or the three of us, a family. But I am used to us as separate courses, like appetizer and dessert, requiring separate plates and flatware. The oddity of this total separateness had not fully occurred to me until that conversation with my friend.

Having divorced parents permanently alters the reality of our world. We form our views of ourselves, of relationships, of family, even of God based on the example of our parents. One child of divorced parents said, "It's basically losing the structure and understanding of your life as you know it. It's like a lot of emotions at once. It changes your life permanently and that is a hard thing to deal with at a young age or at any age."[1] Little wonder, then, that the trauma of a family shattered by divorce lingers on in the broken hearts of those children as they grow into adults.

Not long ago, popular psychology held that children recover from divorce with the same resiliency they display when they bounce back from a broken arm or a knock on the head. One book, originally published in 1989, cheerfully assured parents, "Hopefully it will only take a year for children to come to terms with their basic feelings of loss of the original family and any rejection or desertion by a parent, although some anger and sadness may still persist."[2]

When Judith Wallerstein's book *The Unexpected Legacy of Divorce* came on the scene, Oprah and the rest of the American public uttered a collective gasp and shook their heads in disbelief and well-intended pity for these children of divorce and the ugly, hidden scar tissue they carry. As it turns out, we did not bounce back from the divorce of our parents like brand-new rubber bands. The hurt that was supposed to have been all about our parents somehow left gaping wounds in our own souls, wounds that often festered and turned gangrenous or healed but left deep scars.

Even today there is a happy-go-lucky crowd singing the merry party line of "divorce won't hurt the children if you do it right." Not surprisingly, the proponents of this theory are parents who have divorced. I have yet to meet or hear of a child of divorce who has bought into it—we know better. There is not a "right way" to do divorce so that no one gets hurt. It may be a nice idea, but the reality simply does not work that way. Our actions have consequences, and one of the consequences of divorce is the battered hearts of children whose homes are broken when marriage vows are abandoned.

This book is not intended to be a pity party for children of divorce. It is not a forum to whine about how tragic our lives have been, and it certainly is not a tell-all that airs the dirty laundry of my own family. This is not a sob story about how hard it is to have divorced parents. Rather, it is a story about hope and healing. Coming from a broken home is difficult, but it is not insurmountable. But if all we have are the world's answers to the hurt we experience, then we are in big trouble. It doesn't take long to figure out that the world's answers do not work! There is not enough beer, sex, drugs, perfection, academia, counseling—in short, not enough of anything—to dull the pain, much less heal it.

But there is an answer. God provides a firm foundation for healing our broken hearts.

Finding this foundation became my passion after I was asked to help lead a Sunday school class for children whose parents were divorced or divorcing. At the time, there were no Christian curricula for children of divorce (thankfully that is no longer true), so we used a series of lessons that applied Christian thought to the available secular curricula.

I have no doubt that our lessons made an impact in those children's lives, but when we finished I felt we had let them down. Yes, we had given them some tools and some help, but it simply was not enough. We had used the world's answers with a few supporting Bible verses thrown in for good measure. We had given them a Band-Aid when they needed major surgery. It wasn't that we were not equipped for the major surgery—after all, our God is the Great Physician. We had the answer to the hurt and confusion and anger these children were experiencing. We know the God of the universe, the loving, almighty, awesome God. He is the answer for all our hurts—for the children in that Sunday school class, and for you. He is the answer to every question, the solution to every problem, the end of every quest.

Since then, I have been privileged to talk to others like me, people now in their twenties, thirties and forties whose parents are divorced. Some, like me, were very young when their parents divorced; having a mom and dad who lived separate lives was all they had ever known or could remember. Others were in elementary school or high school or even out of college and living on their own when their families fell apart, leaving them wondering what had happened and upsetting their notions of marriage and commitment. Some had fathers who left, others had mothers who left. Some were from families whose whole lives revolved around church, others were from less-committed families and still others were not part of a faith community at all.

The one thing these grown-up children of divorce have in common is their own faith in God and their assurance that he is working to heal their hearts and provide them with the guidance and strength they need to navigate life as a child of divorce. Each one is not only a child of divorce but also a child of God. This is not to say we have found some spiritual "magic pill" to cure our broken hearts. While we have experienced significant healing and comfort through our faith in God, there remain places where we are still being healed or seeking comfort.

Divorce is not something we simply get over. It is a life-altering fracture in our families, and we continue to deal with the repercussions of that break for the rest of our lives. As we continue on that journey, though, God graciously walks with us, revealing more of his character and his love to us so that we can experience the hope and help we need for whatever part of the journey we are traveling.

The biblical songwriter Asaph had a broken and disillusioned heart when he wrote Psalm 77. In this song, he reflected on how he felt and how God pulled him through it.

I cried out to God for help;
  I cried out to God to hear me.
When I was in distress, I sought the Lord;
  at night I stretched out untiring hands
  and my soul refused to be comforted.
I remembered you, O God, and I groaned;
  I mused, and my spirit grew faint.
You kept my eyes from closing;
  I was too troubled to speak.

I thought about the former days,
    the years of long ago;
I remembered my songs in the night.
    My heart mused and my spirit inquired:
"Will the Lord reject forever?
    Will he never show his favor again?
Has his unfailing love vanished forever?
    Has his promise failed for all time?
Has God forgotten to be merciful?
    Has he in anger withheld his compassion?" (Ps 77:1-9)

That is some pretty raw emotion. Asaph felt alone and abandoned. He remembered a time when life seemed easy and happy, when he sang songs in the night. But that time was long gone. Now he wondered if God would ever love him again, if God could be trusted, if he really was merciful, if his anger had finally won out over his compassion.

One thing I love about the psalms is how real they are. There's no holding back. The psalmists let it all hang out. Many of us would feel guilty saying these words out loud. Question God's love? Sacrilege! And yet there it is, right in the Bible. An honest portrait of a "human merely being" (as e. e. cummings wrote), giving full vent to his despair and disappointment with God.[3]

If that were the end of the story, we might feel vindicated in our doubts but we would not learn how to move beyond doubt to hope. Fortunately, Asaph had more to say:

Then I thought, "To this I will appeal:
    the years of the right hand of the Most High."
I will remember the deeds of the LORD;
    yes, I will remember your miracles of long ago.
I will meditate on all your works
    and consider all your mighty deeds.

Your ways, O God, are holy.
  What god is so great as our God?
You are the God who performs miracles;
  you display your power among the peoples. (Ps 77:10-14)

Asaph had more than just his feelings to rely on. He had the full history of God's deeds, the miracles he had performed long ago. The God Asaph served was the same God who rescued the Israelites out of slavery in Egypt, who made a dry path through the Red Sea (Ex 14:5-31), who fed his people each day with manna and quail (Ex 16), who brought water for them from a rock (Ex 17:1-7). He was the God of the burning bush (Ex 3:1-14) and forty years of hiking in the desert with the same pair of shoes (Deut 29:5) and falling walls in Jericho (Josh 6). He was the God who lovingly cared for and protected his people and who had the power to do so.

Asaph did not sugarcoat his feelings. He had serious questions about God and about God's character. In the end, he decided to trust God *because* of God's character. Even though the circumstances were daunting, Asaph knew who God really was, and that knowledge led him to trust God.

The nineteenth-century theologian, poet and novelist George MacDonald wrote, "Everything depends on the kind of God one believes in."[4] Many of us say we believe in God, but until we know who God is and what he is like, our belief has no substance. What really matters is not the bare fact of God's existence but the kind of God he is. Will he be there when we need him? Does he really love us? Is he involved in our lives, or is he a dispassionate observer? These questions about God's character matter because they determine whether we can rely on him or whether we are simply on our own. When we know God's character, when we know what kind of God he is, our faith becomes a thing of substance.

God has comforted me with the knowledge of his precious and unfailing character. Knowing who he is, through what he tells us about himself in the Bible, has given me confidence in his love and the ability to face life's difficulties, including the fallout from my parents' divorce. My hope is that you find the same peace and wholeness for your heart as we explore together our lives as children of divorce and children of God.

The Trouble
We Have Seen

Every summer I spent a couple of weeks with my dad's parents, after they worked out the details and travel arrangements with my mom. Beginning at age seven, that meant flying alone to visit Grandpa and Ponci (the name that had stuck with my grandma since my toddler years), who lived in central Illinois. I started a vast collection of plastic airline wings, became great friends with flight attendants and learned that the pilots had their own lounges with TVs. Those summer visits were always fun, and they kept me connected to my dad's family. Because I was Ponci and Grandpa's only grandchild, that connection was important both to them and to me.

Ponci and Grandpa lived out in the country in a perfect house that Grandpa built. He was a contractor, so every few years they would buy a different house, fix it up, live in it awhile, then sell it for a tidy profit. The country house was my favorite. It sat on five acres, nestled between fields of corn or soybeans, depending on the crop rotation that year. It caught every summer breeze through its tall windows. You could watch storms approach from miles away and hear the rain on the cornstalks long minutes before it soaked you. When tornado watches were announced, Grandpa and I would stand and watch from the doorway of the garage, just a few short steps from the basement stairs. We could see the funnel clouds form and dissipate, making the eerily green and black sky look like it was boiling upside down. At night, frogs croaked loudly from the pond in the middle of the property. The long, blacktop driveway was perfect for roller-skating, and I was allowed to make forts out of blankets and chairs in the living room.

A few mornings each week, we would meet up with some of Ponci and Grandpa's friends and relatives—Audrey and Engle, Aunt Katie and Uncle Ray, Wayne and Sue—for breakfast at a little country diner, where I got hooked on biscuits with sausage gravy. But Friday mornings, if the weather was good, there was no time for the diner—we had yard sales to visit.

I learned the fine art of bargaining from Ponci, a master sales-woman and negotiator. We would zip around town in her little Triumph convertible, looking for dishes, roller skates or whatever treasure someone else called trash. We would pause for lunch at Taco Bell and maybe stop at the bank to empty the loose change jar into my passbook savings account. But our goal was fixed: We were two cool chicks, Big Ponci and Little Ponci, in search of a twenty-five-cent deal.

I remember one of those trips when I was about nine years old. As we drove around looking for the promising sales we'd circled in the paper that morning, the topic of conversation turned to my mom and dad's divorce. Ponci was gently prying, trying to find out if I was okay. I assured her I was. No need to worry about me—I was fine. I remember Ponci's relief as she said, "Of all the people involved, you handled it the best." Of course, she thought I did everything the best, but the pride in her voice sounded awfully genuine. It was echoed by the pride in my own heart at hearing this—not because I *had* handled things the best, but because she thought I had.

Ponci did not see the times that I woke up screaming and disheveled from violent nightmares when I was four. She did not see the times I cried myself to sleep at age seven because I missed my daddy—and because, as a new Christian, I worried about his salvation, afraid I would be separated from him for eternity. She did not see the gaping hole left in my heart by my dad's absence and apathy. What she saw was a calm, well-behaved, resilient, well-adjusted child. And that is exactly what I wanted her to see. I did not want to be a trouble to anyone. It was far better to go along, to do what I was told, to generally make myself as unnoticeable as possible. Clearly, it was working.

As proud as I was of having fooled Ponci, and presumably many others, I was also profoundly frustrated and disappointed. At our core, we all want to be understood. We want people to "get it," to glimpse the true essence of *us* behind whatever mask we wear. I wore the mask so well that even Big Ponci could not see through it.

This is the story of many who have grown up and provided fodder for the "good divorce" theory. On the outside, we look like we have it together. We are not on drugs, we finished college, we seem like nice people. When I first read Judith Wallerstein's *The Unexpected Legacy of Divorce*, I was overwhelmed with thankfulness that God had drawn me to himself at the age of six and saved me from turning out like some of the women whose stories were told in the book. *Their lives are a mess*, I thought rather arrogantly, thanking God that I did not end up like them (though without Christ, I think I would have).

But that was not the whole story. A few years later Elizabeth Marquardt published *Between Two Worlds*, focusing on the lives of the seemingly fine children of divorce, and I saw myself written all over those pages. Doing well but not daring to hope or trust too much; wanting to protect everyone else while feeling vulnerable and alone; not wanting to cause trouble; being a capable, strong, independent woman who was really doing quite well, thank you very much, please help me.

When Jeff's parents divorced, everyone expected him to keep quiet—about the divorce and about his own feelings. He learned the lesson so well that he was married for ten years before he finally learned to communicate his feelings to his wife. Shortly after his own breakthrough, Jeff found himself in a conversation with a recently divorced coworker. He asked her, "How are your kids doing?"

"Oh, they're doing great," she assured him. "I sat down with each one of them, talked to them about the divorce and asked them how they were feeling. They are all great kids and handling it really well."

"Baloney," Jeff said. "Your kids are lying to you. They're just telling you what you want to hear."

Jeff's blunt reply shocked, even angered, his coworker. But later she sought him out and thanked him. After their last conversation, she confronted her children again and found that Jeff was right. They had been hiding their true feelings, not wanting to hurt her. She immediately signed up the whole family for counseling.

We children of divorce often felt pressured to pretend everything was okay. Sometimes that pressure was overt, but often it was no more than an unspoken hope in the hearts of the adults in our lives. Still, we sensed it and felt the weight of it.

Adults want to believe that kids are tough, that they can handle the strain of divorce. Popular psychology reinforced this idea for a long time—and some psychologists still do—for the same reasons that doctors tell parents that their young children cannot feel the pain of a medical procedure: it is too painful for us to hurt a child and not be able to explain or ease the pain, so we pretend they cannot feel it.

Some of our parents may have felt that same kind of helplessness and anguish, particularly if they were in a violent marriage or if they were abandoned. Some knew it would be painful for us, but they believed it was also the best thing. Only a third of divorces are the result of high-conflict marriages in which violence was likely,[1] but since the 1970s, when no-fault divorce became the norm, one spouse cannot *make* the other stay. A mom or dad who is left behind like that tries to make the best of a bad situation, often while blindly groping through their own fog of emotional pain. And as the children of such parents, we wanted to protect them and make them believe they were succeeding. Elizabeth Marquardt found that more than half of us, compared to just a third of children from intact homes, felt a particular need to protect our mothers. Judith Wallerstein observed similar patterns, telling parents that even very young children will "do anything to not rock the boat because they love you and want to take care of you, and they realize that this is a crisis for at least one of you."[2]

We did such a good job pretending to be fine that everyone believed us. Alison Clarke-Stewart, coauthor of *Divorce: Causes and Consequences*, remarked, "That was one of the surprising things in the literature and also in our conversations with the students taking our class, that parents don't seem to realize how much their children are suffering."[3]

Now that we are adults, we are supposed to be long over the split that happened in our family so many years ago, or old enough to realize that these things just happen. One young woman wrote to advice columnist "Dear Abby" about her parents' divorce, announced two weeks before her own wedding: "I am 28 years old and should be able to handle the news but I cannot. I have been devastated by the end of a marriage that I thought was a good one until only a few months ago."[4]

Divorce is heartbreaking. As children, we were often caught in the middle of our own emotions and the hopes of our parents and other adults around us. Many of us felt overlooked and misunderstood, and many of us still feel that no one is aware of the sadness we carry around from our parents' divorce. In one sense, we are right. No human can ever really know or fully understand the wounds on our souls. But God can. He created us, and he is very aware when we hurt.

Psalm 56:8 says, "You keep track of all my sorrows. / You have collected all my tears in your bottle. / You have recorded each one in your book" (NLT). Some biblical commentators think the psalmist is alluding here to *lachrymatories*, tear bottles that were popular in Roman times. The bottles were used to collect the tears of funeral mourners, which were then stored with the body, showing how precious and loved the deceased person had been by how full the tear bottles were. Sometimes people would use the bottles to catch and store the tears of a loved one who was suffering and near death, commemorating the deceased's final anguish.

Other commentators, however, including the nineteenth-century Baptist preacher Charles Spurgeon, discredit this theory. They contend that there is no evidence of tear bottles being used in pre-Roman Jewish culture. Instead, they suggest that the allusion is to fine wine. In fact, the NIV offers an alternate translation that reads "put my tears in your wineskin." The image here is of a vintner who plants vineyards and takes vigilant care of his tender vines; when the harvest time comes, he removes the grapes from their vines and places them in a winepress. There they are squeezed until they have released every drop of their juice, which is then stored in wineskins (leather bottles), to be poured out at a later time.

In either case, the implication is the same. Whether our bottles of tears are lachrymatories, bearing witness of how loved and special we are, or whether they are wineskins, storing the meticulously cultivated and purposefully pressed out fruit of our lives—God is in the process. He is taking special, tender care of our pain, and he is careful not to waste it or regard it casually.

He keeps track of *all* your sorrows. Not just some—*all*, the psalmist says. What a precious thought! This is no mild brushoff, but a "tender concern" as seventeenth-century English pastor Matthew Henry noted in his commentary on the psalms.[5]

I tend to keep diaries only when I am sad or distressed. When things are going well or even just okay, I have more important tasks than pouring my heart out on even the prettiest of journal pages. Life is to be lived, not simply recorded. But when I am sad, I cannot wait to let loose every raw feeling within the pages of a diary, where I feel free to express myself. Yet my journals do not capture all my sorrows, but only those I felt burdened with, when I had time on my hands and the energy to write and a pen nearby. At best, my journals represent only a haphazard collection of woes. But God has been carefully keeping track of each one. I can imagine him saying to me in heaven one day, "Do you remember the time when you cried about ____?" And I will reply, "No, I don't remember that one. Did I really cry about that?" According to the psalmist, all he will have to do is turn to his record book and say, "See? I wrote it all down right here."

Bill Hybels, founder and senior pastor of Willow Creek Community Church in the suburbs of Chicago, talks about this passage in his book *The God You're Looking For:*

> Every person is wounded in one way or another. . . . [God] was there, and He didn't miss a millisecond of what took place. . . . You must grab hold of the secure lifeline provided by the truth that *God knows*. He is *intimately* acquainted with all your ways. He doesn't watch you from a distance. No feeling, no hurt, no scar, no wound has ever escaped His notice. Not only does He know, He cares. The Psalms declare, "You have seen me tossing and turning through the night"—let this next phrase sink in—"You have collected all my tears and preserved them in your bottle! You have recorded every one

in your book." . . . How do you like that? When God greets us in heaven, He'll be able to wave our tear bottle in front of His smiling face. "Didn't miss a one," He'll say. "Not a single one." Additionally, He not only collects each tear but also records each one in a book. . . . God is never careless with your tears, hurts, and wounds. That's how much you matter to Him.[6]

Even when it seems that no one else knows what we are going through or cares about our sadness, God knows. Our tears are precious to him because we are precious to him!

IS IT OKAY TO BE SAD?

There is a story in the Bible about a woman named Hannah who was unable to have children. Her husband's other wife had a full brood and liked to make fun of Hannah; Hannah, having kept her girlish figure and sweet temperament (I like to think), was their husband's favorite. Poor Hannah was heartbroken and miserable. In a culture that defined womanhood by motherhood, Hannah was seen as abandoned by God, and she felt that way herself.

Hannah was seriously depressed. The Bible says she could not eat because she was so miserable. Her husband, Elkanah, who loved her dearly, tried to cheer her by asking, "Don't I mean more to you than ten sons?" (1 Sam 1:8). But even a doting husband was little comfort. Hannah was inconsolable. When Elkanah went to the tabernacle to worship God, Hannah accompanied him. There she poured out her heart before God, weeping in "bitterness of soul" (1 Sam 1:10). Her display of sorrow was so uninhibited that the priest, Eli, actually thought she was drunk!

Children of divorce face subtle and sometimes not-so-subtle pressure to move on. Mom left Dad for an exciting new life, and your sadness puts a damper on her newfound enthusiasm. Or Granny and Gramps disapproved of your father, that bum, and think everyone should be heartily glad he is gone. Your teachers worried that you should see a counselor. And now that you're grown, people wonder why you can't just get over it already. Sometimes you wonder that yourself.

Few of those people would have made you climb the jungle gym still sporting bandages from a fresh concussion around your head, and few would have expected you to run the fifty-yard dash on crutches. But the wounds of a child of divorce are not wrapped in visible bandages. It is easy to forget the wounds are there—even for the child who has them! It's easier to sweep them under the rug, to suck it up and appear heroic.

All too often the church gives us this same message. If you have Jesus in your life but you are still hurting, still reeling with pain, still aching in some dull spot, you obviously do not have enough faith. After all, Jesus came that we might have life, and more abundantly! That is the message a lot of churches dole out, and it is a very unsatisfying answer for those whose hearts are still broken.

Yes, Jesus has come that we might have abundant life, but that does not mean all our problems will go away. In fact, Jesus promised his disciples that they would have trouble. One translation is even more direct: "You will have to suffer" (Jn 16:33 CEV). We still live in a world filled with sin and all its consequences—illness, death, war, poverty, heartbreak—and divorce. There is a reason the Bible talks about heaven as a place where "God will wipe away every tear from their eyes" (Rev 7:17); until we get there, we will always be dealing with sadness and pain and disappointment.

Hannah, the disconsolate wife crying in the Temple, was not condemned for her emotions. The priest, after realizing that she was drowning in sorrow and not booze, compassionately said, "Go in peace, and may the God of Israel grant you what you have asked of him" (1 Sam 1:17). He did not tell her to pull herself together, to act like a good Israelite and pretend everything was okay. Instead, he blessed her, acknowledged her pain and joined with her in praying for God's merciful relief.

Jesus is not about sound bites, platitudes and feel-good talk shows. I suspect that Christians who like to hand out slogan-style assurances either have never experienced real pain or, more likely, never faced their pain and allowed God to begin to heal them. Jesus is not afraid of our sorrow. Isaiah called him "a man of sorrows, and familiar with suffering" (Is 53:3).

That famous verse "Jesus wept" (Jn 11:35) occurs in the context of Jesus' sorrow over the death of his friend Lazarus. Jesus knew as soon as he heard of his friend's illness that he would raise Lazarus from the dead. He hinted of his plan twice to his disciples. But because they were always slow to grasp the miraculous in the flesh-and-blood man they saw before them each day, he told them plainly, "Lazarus is dead" (Jn 11:14), and he made it clear that he would raise him from the dead. Yet when they arrived in Bethany, Jesus cried real tears.

Perhaps these were tears of pity for the sorrow of Lazarus's sisters and friends, who did not yet know that their loved one would soon be alive again. John says Jesus' spirit was troubled when he saw his friends Mary and Martha crying for their brother, and all the relatives and neighbors mourning along with them. Perhaps these were tears of anger over the injustice and tyranny of death itself, a result of humanity's fall into sin and Satan's stranglehold on this world. John says Jesus was again "deeply moved" (11:38) as he neared the cave that was Lazarus's grave. Whatever the cause of the tears, the fact is that he wept, plain and simple.

In the garden of Gethsemane, Jesus told his disciples, "My soul is overwhelmed with sorrow to the point of death" (Mt 26:38). That night, Christ wept, pleaded with God and sweated drops of blood. The One who is called the Life, the Bread of Life, the Living Water, the Everlasting—the One who had always lived—was about to die. Death, the antithesis of everything Jesus is, was about to consume him. His sorrow was real, so real that we shy away from it. We do not like to picture Jesus prostrate and weeping. It is uncomfortable and untidy. The most popular artists' renditions of this scene show Christ bathed in an aura of golden light, kneeling by a rock, hands folded primly, eyes lifted beseechingly to heaven. But Scripture shows us our Savior stretched out on the ground, a posture of total abandonment, a broken, forlorn figure (Mt 26:39; Mk 14:35). God gives us this vivid picture of our Lord to remind us that he knows the messy, broken, unbeautiful reality of our own sorrows.

There is another reason we are given these glimpses into our Savior's sorrow. Jesus "had to be made like his brothers in every way, in order that he might become a merciful and faithful high priest" (Heb 2:17). Jesus felt deep pain, and not just the physical pain of dying on the cross. He felt deep emotional pain as well. His heart was troubled and broken, and he cried.

If Jesus can cry uninhibitedly, then so can we. There is no shame or guilt in feeling sad. God honors our emotions and does not ask us to hold back. He knows we are hurting, and he wants to use our times of deep emotion to teach us about himself, to show us that he is faithful even when our hearts are full of grief.

God is not afraid of our sorrow. He does not expect us to sweep it under the rug. He knows about it, and he wants to see us through it, not around it. The psalmist wrote, "Even though I walk / through the valley of the shadow of death, / I will fear no evil, / for you are with me" (Ps 23:4). We do not like valleys; we want to find an alternate route. Our culture is all about avoiding pain. Turn on the television and see how long it is before you see a commercial for a prescription medication to treat depression or anxiety. Of course, there are legitimate cases when medical intervention is necessary for mental and emotional pain. Chemical or hormonal changes can make a person feel despondent or stressed for no external reason, and this kind of imbalance needs medical intervention. But when something terribly sad has happened to us, it is only logical that we will feel pain. Dr. Neil Kalter pointed this out when he wrote that children of divorce "will not be 'unnecessarily' sad or distressed, they will be *normally* sad and distressed."[7] God does not promise to take away our pain—at least not immediately—but he does promise to walk with us through our pain.

Psalm 34:18 says, "The LORD is close to the brokenhearted / and saves those who are crushed in spirit." Psalm 147:3 says, "He heals the brokenhearted / and binds up their wounds." When we feel wounded and crushed, we can be assured that God is gently laboring over us, healing our brokenness, binding our hurts. Like a mother kissing away the owies or a nurse gently cleansing a wound, God knows what our broken hearts need for healing to come, and he himself is the salve.

I used to work at a Christian ministry where we often received books that publishers or authors wanted us to promote or review. At one particularly low point in my life, when God seemed distant and my situation felt hopeless, a copy of a new book landed on my desk. It was intended for people who were unfamiliar with the Christian faith, and it examined the character of God. It was not especially deep or hard-hitting. But at a time when I felt brokenhearted, that simple and gentle reminder about God's presence and character was just what I needed. As I read that book and remembered what God was really like, I began to see past my present situation and feel the tattered edges of my heart start to heal. God's character was the bandage that held me together.

NO WORDS TO PRAY

When we feel so burdened that we do not know what to pray, the Holy Spirit actually prays for us! In Romans 8:26, Paul tells us, "The Spirit helps us in our weakness. We do not know what we ought to pray for, but the Spirit himself intercedes for us with groans that words cannot express."

I like to collect quotes. Whenever I read something that strikes me as profound, I copy it into a journal. One of my favorite quotes is from Zora Neale Hurston's book *Their Eyes Were Watching God*. She writes, "There is a basin in the mind where words float around on thought and thought on sound and sight. Then there is a depth of thought untouched by words, and deeper still a gulf of formless feelings untouched by thought."[8] When our pain submerges to that "gulf of formless feelings," we can feel helpless and impotent in prayer. But it is at these times, through the Spirit's intercession in "groans that words cannot express," that our most beautiful prayers rise to heaven.

Sometimes it helps to have a friend praying for you, to know that another person is carrying the weight of your spiritual numbness when you are unable to do so yourself. During a dark time in my own life, my dear friend Deb committed to praying for me daily. I had broken up with a boyfriend, a man I had fallen hopelessly in love with. In the end I felt abandoned just the way I had when my dad cut off all contact with me. I was devastated. How could God let me feel the same pain twice? Couldn't he at least pick a different pain to inflict on me? I spiraled downward, unable to eat, barely able to function, aware that I was holding on to my sanity by the thinnest of threads. I had been sad before, but this was different. It seemed to dredge up every hurt feeling I had ever known, all at the same time. In the midst of this struggle, I was unable to see God. I knew he was there, but that was as far as I could get.

Deeply depressed, I was at a point where many of us have been (or will be) sometime in our spiritual journeys. I prayed and felt nothing, heard nothing. I was worse than numb, worse than deaf. I felt like I was dead inside. And I knew that I needed prayer, but my soul was so overcome by this nothing that I had no words to pray, no thoughts, no feelings. So Deb took my life before God's throne for me. Every day she prayed for me, and she reminded me often that she was praying for me. She did this for a full year.

Deb carried me through those dark days and darker nights with her prayers. Looking back on it now, it almost appears in my mind like a scene from John Bunyan's classic Christian allegory, *Pilgrim's Progress*. I was Pilgrim, half dead from a beating by Ruthless World, but mercifully being carried to safety on the back of beautiful Intercession.

If you are in a similar desert of the soul, ask a trusted friend to commit to praying for you, like Deb did for me. Someday you may return the favor for another weary soul. In fact, that is what Deb was doing. She had walked through that valley of depression and numb spiritual emptiness years earlier. Several women to whom she was very close committed to praying for her every day until the darkness lifted from her soul. Their intercession on her behalf enabled her to move beyond the valley. Today Deb has a reputation as a faithful and committed intercessor for those in need.

BLESSINGS IN SORROW

Jesus tells us in Matthew 5:4, "Blessed are those who mourn, for they will be comforted." I learned that verse as a child. It was one of the "Be Attitudes" (a cute take on the Beatitudes), illustrated with a black-and-yellow paper bumblebee. And that is how Christians often approach these verses. We want to buzz into people's pain, stick a Beatitude on them and hope they feel better. We are like the Christians James chastised with these words: "Suppose a brother or sister is without clothes and daily food. If one of you says to him, 'Go, I wish you well; keep warm and well fed,' but does nothing about his physical needs, what good is it?" (2:15-16).

Matthew 5:4 is not a pat, "cheer up, tomorrow is another day" answer to sorrow. When we treat it that way, we are missing the point. It is a hint at the later revelation of a Comforter, a Spirit who will indwell us and bring peace to our battered souls. Paul explains the comfort we receive from God through the Holy Spirit—and what we are to do with it—in greater depth: "Praise be to the God and Father of our Lord Jesus Christ, the Father of compassion and the God of all comfort, who comforts us in all our troubles, so that we can comfort those in any trouble with the comfort we ourselves have received from God" (2 Cor 1:3-4).

We did not choose to be children of divorce, to have our families ripped apart, to have Mom and Dad living in separate homes. We would never have chosen this. But finding ourselves in this situation, we do have a choice to make. Will we allow God to comfort us? And will we offer that same comfort to others who are hurting?

Those of us now in our twenties and thirties are the first generations to reach adulthood since divorce became the norm in our society. We are just now finding our voices, expressing our hurts and helping each other heal. As God heals our hearts, he can use our sorrows and our stories to bring healing into the lives of others. Remember, he saves each tear in a bottle—that is not the work of a wasteful God.

God knows our sorrow intimately because he made us and knows everything about us. He has experienced great sorrow himself, and in the Bible he lets us see the depths of his grief. He promises to heal our broken hearts and be with us in the process. He prays for us when we are too worn out with grief to form words. He gives comfort to our souls through his Holy Spirit.

R. C. Sproul said, "If believers really understood the character and personality and the nature of God, it would revolutionize their lives."[9] Knowing that God cares for us means that we do not have to suffer in silence. We do not have to hide our sorrow or pretend that everything is just fine. We can acknowledge our sadness over the breakup of our family and begin to experience God's grace as we begin to know the tender, compassionate way that our God cares for us and shares in our sorrow.

Faith(fulness) of
Our Fathers

By the time I finished elementary school, I was a seasoned traveler and well on my way to calling airports my second home. I moved so confidently through the concourses that adults would stop me to ask directions. Still, my first trip to Los Angeles the summer I was thirteen tested my mettle.

It was a nonstop flight from Newark to LAX, so even though I was too old to have a flight attendant take me wherever I needed to go, the trip was a piece of cake—until I landed in Los Angeles and could not find my father. The plane taxied into a small outlying terminal with only a few gates, so Dad should have been easy to spot, but he simply was not there. At first I laughed it off; he was always late. I bonded with the gate agent, a burly black man with a moustache. He was a father himself and refused to leave until he saw me safely in someone's care. When an hour had gone by and I was still sitting there alone, the gate agent began to worry, and my hope began to wane. The gate agent called Dad's home, where there was no answer, and then his work, where his coworkers insisted my visit was all he could talk about, so he could not have forgotten.

As it turned out, airport construction for the summer Olympics, which were to be held in Los Angeles the following year, turned the fifteen-minute drive between terminals into a two-hour traffic jam. Dad had been on his way the whole time.

The trouble was—whether I was waiting for a birthday card, a phone call or a visit—I never knew if Dad would come through. He would send an extravagant gift one year, like the giant stuffed turtle nearly as big as me that he sent when I was seven or eight, and then the next year he would neglect to even send a card. I learned to live in the moment, to accept the joys of this day, this minute, while coolly adopting a "wait and see" attitude toward the future.

I visited Dad twice more in Los Angeles during my teen years. Together we went to Disneyland and San Francisco and Las Vegas and San Diego. We got sunburned at the beach and looked at movie stars' houses. We ate at the Hard Rock Café, watched roller skaters in Venice and walked the Hollywood Walk of Fame. After dark we drove up into the Hollywood Hills to see the lights of Los Angeles, the famous intersection of Hollywood and Vine laid out in the valley below us as clearly as the Big Dipper in a midnight sky. At night I slept on a futon in a room where I could see the postgame fireworks from Dodger Stadium.

The last visit was when I was seventeen. We had a good time together, I thought. Dad, who was just then fulfilling his dream of working in the movie business, had to work most of the time I was there, but we managed some weekend trips. Ponci and Grandpa were there with Ponci's sister, Aunt Mart, for part of the time. When the visit was over, Dad and his second wife took me to the airport. We said goodbye, said we loved each other, hugged and kissed. Then I got on a plane and did not hear from or talk to my dad for eight years.

It took me a long time to realize that Dad was intentionally avoiding contact with me. I wrote him letters and heard nothing back. He had always been so unreliable, I figured he was just procrastinating as usual. But when Christmas and then my birthday came and went without a word from him, I realized this was more than casual forgetfulness—it was purposeful abandonment. My letters became angry, then desperate, and then I stopped trying and began to accept that this was the new reality with my dad: estrangement.

Almost a decade went by before I saw Dad again, at his brother's second wedding in Chicago when I was twenty-five. Dad's family was too small for him to avoid me, and though I was wary, I had no desire to avoid him. We spoke politely, and a few months later when he was researching a screenplay in the Washington, D.C., suburbs where I live, he took me to dinner. We began the slow process of rebuilding our relationship, but even today I do not count on my dad. I am always happy to see him or hear from him, but I no longer expect those things. They are welcome bonuses when they do happen, but as long as I am not anticipating them, I will not be disappointed if Dad does not come through. I love my dad, but I do not trust him to not let me down.

Children of divorce have a love-hate relationship with trust. On the one hand, Generation X has a reputation for cynicism, skepticism and apathy. A *Newsweek* article from the mid-1990s on Nirvana's lead singer and songwriter Kurt Cobain observed, "Grunge is what happens when children of divorce get their hands on guitars."[1] The music of our generation was not about peace, love and happiness. It was about alienation, abandonment and discontent. On the other hand, Generations X and Y live our lives online and out in the open, vulnerable to strangers in a way that makes most of our elders squirm with discomfort.

Jen Abbas explained it this way in her book *Generation Ex:* "Our longing for belonging is an innate and undeniable part of our makeup, but our family's failure to give us consistent connection can warp our framework for intimacy. Our fears of being dismissed, let down, betrayed, abandoned, or rejected stifle our willingness to risk authenticity and vulnerability as an adult. We send mixed 'Come here!/Go away!' signals as we vacillate between our conflicting impulses of revelation and restraint."[2]

In other words, we are so desperate for real intimacy and emotional safety, and at the same time so afraid that we will never find either, that we alternately hold back too much and reveal too much of ourselves. We find it difficult to strike a healthy balance between knowing when we can open up, trusting someone else with our heart and deepest longings, and knowing when we should be discreet, reserving our thoughts and emotions for a time and a place and a person who is genuinely trustworthy.

Part of our struggle with trust stems from the broken trust with our parents. The people who were supposed to model and teach us concepts like trustworthiness, honesty and faithfulness are instead the people who have let us down the most, lied to us most consistently and failed to be there when we most needed them. While their actions were often unintentional, we had front-row seats to observe their failures, and it left many of us with doubts about who can be trusted.

That doubt can extend to our relationship with God. It is one of the mysteries of faith that we learn so much about God from our earthly fathers. God is referred to as our Father in Scripture, and the reference is meant to identify the intimate, dependent relationship we have with him. For children of divorce, though, this metaphor for God is more than a little problematic.

The majority of us have watched our fathers leave,[3] watched them break their promises, watched them in their worst moments. We have learned not to rely on them, to live without them, to make it on our own because they cannot be counted on. Without even realizing it, we can begin to place this same kind of instinctive doubt on our relationship with God. We expect him to let us down when the going gets tough, or we wonder if he even exists.

I find this unwarranted doubt creeping into my own expectations of God, despite my best efforts to the contrary. A pious expression of God's sovereignty—"thy will be done"—becomes an easy out for the disappointment I sometimes secretly expect from my Lord. That low expectation is based on my own sinful fear of trusting God's love and faithfulness. Like Satan's lie to Eve—"Did God really say . . . ?" (Gen 3:1)—the very subtlety of it makes it a dangerous poison, hard to detect but deadly to the soul. It sounds good to say that God is sovereign—and indeed he is. But when I make his sovereignty a cloak for my feelings that he has somehow let me down, I overstep the boundaries of his character and make him out to be something he is not.

God does not need my easy out. He is not a God of disappointment; he is a God of "immeasurably more than all we ask or imagine" (Eph 3:20). God goes above and beyond. He is not just sitting around fulfilling orders in a heavenly warehouse as we pray. He is actively working to give us everything we need, even those things we never realized we needed or those things that seemed like too much to ask for. Not only will God always be faithful, he will go above and beyond my wildest imaginations. He is extravagant in his faithfulness. Even when things do not look very promising, he is working in mighty ways. The trick is to get beyond how things look and see how they really are.

WHERE GOD HAS JUST BEEN

Moses had one of the closest relationships with God of any person who ever lived. God picked him to lead Israel out of slavery in Egypt, appeared dramatically before him in a burning bush, parted the Red Sea with his staff, then proceeded to rain down manna and quail and bring water from rocks in the desert. In the midst of all this, Moses went up on Mount Sinai and received the Ten Commandments from God. In the biblical account in Exodus (and in the classic movie starring Charlton Heston), Moses came down from the mountain after this holy, reverential time with God to find a full-blown frat party taking place in the Israelite camp (Ex 32). The people had gone crazy, making a gold calf to worship, and carousing and drinking. Moses got so mad that in utter frustration he threw down the stone tablets he was carrying.

Moses had just had the ultimate mountaintop experience—literally. God had spoken to him and given him specific instructions for how the people were to live and worship him. What a spiritual high! And then it all came crashing down when Moses saw how quickly and easily the people had abandoned God. Discouraged and alone, Moses had one of the most amazing exchanges with God in all of Scripture (Ex 33:12-23). God assured Moses that he would go with the people and lead them into the Promised Land. Moses, needing more encouragement, asked to see God's glory, and God agreed! He would cause all of his goodness to pass in front of Moses, and he would proclaim his name, "the LORD," in Moses' presence. There was a nice Moses-sized hole in a rock nearby, and God covered Moses with his hand while he passed by, letting Moses see his back.

In his book *Velvet Elvis*, Rob Bell, founding pastor of Mars Hill Bible Church in Grand Rapids, Michigan, says Jewish rabbis speculated that the phrase "you will see my back" was a euphemism for "where I just was." In other words, while Moses could not see in front of God, he could see the view behind him. He could see where God's footsteps had fallen along the path.[4]

Isn't that how we often experience God? There are few things we know about the future, and what we do know are only some of the big ideas: new heavens and a new earth (Is 65:17; Rev 21:1), streets of gold (Rev 21:21), a big house with many rooms (Jn 14:2).

But when we look back at our lives, we can see God in the details. The random way we met our friends, the odd decisions that saved our lives, the bizarre circumstances that led us here—when we look back from the perspective of today, we can see God's footprints and his ordered hand in all these seemingly accidental occurrences.

When we look for God at work in our everyday lives, we find him there. Anne had prayed over every detail of her upcoming wedding, and every piece had fallen into place except one. She was just weeks away from the big day and still had not found earrings to match the necklace her mother and grandmother had both worn in their weddings. While shopping with a friend, Anne saw the perfect pair and spontaneously uttered a loud "Praise God!" Her friend rolled her eyes and said, "Come on, God did not do that!" But Anne was certain he had. She had disciplined herself to look for God at work, even in the small things. This discipline allowed her to see God's hand over and over and kept her confident that he would continue to work out even the minutest details of her wedding.

Anne's ability to see God in the everyday is a discipline practiced by her whole family. When Anne's infant nephew was diagnosed with a debilitating and life-threatening brain tumor, Anne's sister-in-law Julie began a series of e-mail updates to family and friends that made their way across the country and around the world. Julie detailed the latest medical treatments, the small triumphs and setbacks, and the everyday joys that redefined her notions of motherhood. Whether she and her husband were entertaining a bored eighteen-month-old for hours on end while waiting for their doctor appointment, or wondering whether the latest fever was the flu or a dangerous infection, or praying for God to let their baby's eyesight return, Julie's e-mails always focused on the good things God was doing in their lives. While others might have looked at their situation and wondered where God was, Julie and the rest of her family saw God right in the midst of their pain and worry.

If you have difficulty seeing God's footprints along your path, you are not alone. All through the Psalms, David and Asaph talk about feeling lonely and afraid and forgotten. "Why, O LORD, do you stand far off? / Why do you hide yourself in times of trouble?" (Ps 10:1). "How long, O LORD? Will you forget me forever? / How long will you hide your face from me? / How long must I wrestle with my thoughts / and every day have sorrow in my heart? / How long will my enemy triumph over me?" (Ps 13:1-2). Charles Spurgeon said Psalm 13, sometimes known as the "How Long Psalm," could just as easily be called the "Howling Psalm."[5] It is a full-on lament for God's presence.

C. J. Mahaney, founder of Sovereign Grace Ministries, is sympathetic with David's feelings of abandonment. He writes, "Our common tendency is to habitually begin with the internal, the subjective, the experiential, then use those feelings and impressions to determine what we'll accept as being objective fact. We let our feelings tell us what's true, instead of letting the truth transform our feelings."[6]

God never forgot David. It just felt that way in the present moment. In fact, when we think of David, we think of a man who enjoyed God's favor, who was called a man after God's own heart (1 Sam 13:14). What David's songwriting shows us is that even he, God's chosen king and favored one, had to discipline himself to see God's faithfulness when circumstances tempted him to doubt. And looking back on David's life, we have to admit that God was faithful to him. He chose David, though everyone else thought he was beyond notice, to be the future king of Israel (1 Sam 16:1-13). He caused David to defeat the feared enemy Goliath when David was still a boy too young to be a warrior (1 Sam 17). He preserved David's life over and over again from the murderous hand of King Saul (1 Sam 18—19). He made David king of Israel and promised to establish his throne forever (2 Sam 7:14-16), a promise fulfilled through Christ (Heb 1:5-9). Even when

David sinned with Bathsheba, God sent Nathan to convict David and restore him through repentance (2 Sam 11—12).

David did not always feel the truth of God's faithfulness. Sometimes in the fog of the moment he felt abandoned and forgotten. But he never was. His feelings lied to him, just as ours can do. When our parents let us down, we can feel like God has let us down, but he has not. When our circumstances crush us, we can feel like God has deserted us, like we are on our own, thrown to the wolves, abandoned. But we are not abandoned. If, like David, we remember that faithfulness is part of God's character, and we practice the discipline of seeing God at work, we will be able to trust him in spite of our feelings.

GOD WILL NOT DESERT US

Lynn's parents were both Christians, so she thought she was safe from the upheaval of divorce. She had seen her friends and classmates go through their parents' divorces, and was glad she did not have to worry about that with her family. So when her parents split up during her sophomore year of high school, Lynn was devastated. Her older brother headed off to college, leaving her to deal with her parents alone. To make things worse, Lynn had to decide whether to live with her mom or dad. Although she had never been close to her father, Lynn could not stand the idea of living with her mother and her mom's new boyfriend. She was convinced their relationship was adulterous. When Lynn announced her intention to live with her father instead, her mother felt betrayed and angrily told her to get out. Lynn had little contact with her mother after that.

Determined not to be a victim, Lynn went stoically through her teen years. Not until she was in her twenties, married and the mother of her own child did Lynn finally grieve the loss of her family, especially the loss of her mother.

Journalist Brooke Lea Foster, writing of her own experience as the child of divorced parents, wrote, "While we may blame a father for breaking up our family when he initiates a divorce, we may forgive him more easily than a mother in the same situation. A mother isn't supposed to just walk away from family."[7] After all, our mothers carried us inside their bodies for nine long months, nurturing and sustaining us until we were ready to enter the world.

Scripture affirms the unlikelihood of a mother's abandonment. In Isaiah 49:15, God said to his people, "Can a mother forget the baby at her breast / and have no compassion on the child she has borne?" The implied answer is, of course not! How could such a thing happen? Who could imagine it? Yet if we can imagine it—if we have lived it—there is still hope. Isaiah goes on to record God's promise: "Though she may forget, / I will not forget you!" And he does not stop there. God says, "See, I have engraved you on the palms of my hands" (Is 49:16). Every time God opens his hand to take action, he sees us there. He has put us in a place of prominence, where he will always be reminded of us and will never forget us. We can be sure that this promise applies to all believers, not just the people to whom Isaiah's prophecy was given in the sixth century B.C.; Jesus carried the wounds from his crucifixion for our sins in his hands and feet and side, even after his resurrection (Jn 20:27). In Jesus' glorified, perfect body, those wounds are an eternal reminder of God's love for us, permanently etched in the palms of his hands.

Unfortunately, people do desert us sometimes—even mothers. And it can certainly feel like God has deserted us, especially when everything seems to be going wrong. When the car breaks down, a friend is diagnosed with cancer or a promotion does not materialize, we may wonder where God is. But the truth, the absolute reality, is that he never deserts us.

After God led the Israelites out of Egypt, they still had a big job ahead of them: conquering the land God promised to give them, a land reported to be filled with giants and warriors. At the beginning of their journey, Moses sent twelve men into the Promised Land on a reconnaissance mission (Num 13). Two of them, Joshua and Caleb, came back filled with wonder at the giant fruit and lush pasture of the land, confident that God would give them victory. The other ten saw only fortified cities, strong warriors and an impossible task destined to fail. Sure, there were grape clusters so big two men were needed to carry them. But what good were those grapes if the people who owned the vineyards could crush you underfoot? The people gave in to fear and listened to the ten naysayers. So God sentenced them to wander in the desert for forty long years (Num 14:26-35).

After the forty years were up, it was time to enter the Promised Land. The cities were not any less fortified, and the warriors living in the land were not any weaker. The Israelites were scared and needed reassurance that God would be with them, even though they should have known by then that God is faithful. During their wilderness wanderings, they had depended on God for daily food and water, and he had not let them down once. Every day, a fresh batch of manna appeared on the ground; every day, new flocks of quail flew in. Moses reminded the people, "[God] has watched over your journey through this vast desert. These forty years the LORD your God has been with you, and you have not lacked anything" (Deut 2:7). But God did not mock or chastise his people for their fear. Instead, he encouraged and reassured them: "The LORD himself goes before you and will be with you; he will never leave you nor forsake you. Do not be afraid; do not be discouraged" (Deut 31:8).

It is easy to get discouraged when we feel abandoned and alone. Elisha was a prophet of God in the Old Testament. He became the target of the king of Aram after it was discovered that Elisha was tipping off the king of Israel whenever an attack was planned against him. The king of Aram sent his army to surround the town where Elisha was staying, intending to capture and kill this too-accurate prophet.

When Elisha's servant got up that morning and saw the horses and chariots of the Aramean king encircling their hideout, he understandably panicked. Elisha, however, was not worried. What did he see that the servant did not? In this case, it was something tangible. Elisha prayed that God would open the servant's eyes and let him see what Elisha could see. God granted Elisha's request, and suddenly the servant saw that the hills were full not only of the horses and chariots of the king of Aram but of horses and chariots of fire—the army of God. Elisha calmly told his servant, "Those who are with us are more than those who are with them" (2 Kings 6:16). In other words, the enemy is outnumbered. We are on the winning side. God has not abandoned us.

From a human perspective, Elisha's servant saw only the danger facing them. Until God opened the servant's eyes, he could not see the armies of God surrounding them, ready to do battle and protect him and Elisha. They were not abandoned. God was there the whole time.

There is no fear with God. He knows what is ahead, and yet he is with us in the moment. He will always be with us. He will not take a quick nap or sneak off to watch over someone more important. He will never leave us or forsake us. Ever.

We can trust someone who is always there, someone who never leaves. Psalm 9:10 puts it this way: "Those who know your name will trust in you, / for you, LORD, have never forsaken those who seek you." God has a proven track record of trustworthiness that is thousands of years long. In his commentary on this verse, Matthew Henry had this to say:

> The better God is known the more he is trusted. Those who know him to be a God of infinite wisdom will trust him *further than they can see him* (Job 35:14); those who know him to be a God of almighty power will trust him when creature-

confidences fail and they have nothing else to trust to (2 Chr. 20:12); and those who know him to be a God of infinite grace and goodness will trust him *though he slay them*, Job 13:15. Those who know him to be a God of inviolable truth and faithfulness will rejoice in his word of promise, and rest upon that, though performance be deferred and intermediate providences seem to contradict it.[8]

GOD KEEPS HIS PROMISES

We hear a lot about promises these days. There are promise rings, worn by Christian teenagers who have taken a vow of chastity. Every election cycle there are campaign promises, when candidates assert what they will or will not do if elected to office. There are the Promise Keepers, a group started in the 1990s by some men in Colorado. It is a Christian movement that helps men learn how to become promise keepers within their families, and form accountability groups to follow through. These men know that the idea of a human promise keeper is based on the promise-keeping nature of God.

Imagine yourself at the head of a large religious organization, which you took over when the founder retired many years ago. Though you were young and unsure at the time, the founder had taught you to look to God for help and guidance and to follow God's leading. Over the decades, you have seen the organization grow through good times and bad. Now, years later, it is your turn to step aside and pass the reins to someone younger. What words of wisdom will you impart to that person?

This was Joshua's task. He was Moses' protégé after proving that he was a man who believed and followed God. He was one of the two spies who brought back a good report about the Promised Land. Now, after leading Israel on a successful campaign to take possession of the land, including a particularly glorious battle that involved a lot of marching, trumpets and walls spontaneously falling down, it was Joshua's turn to enter that other promised land—heaven.

Joshua had some final words for the leaders of Israel before he left "to go the way of all the earth: You know with all your heart and soul that not one of all the good promises the LORD your God gave you has failed. Every promise has been fulfilled; not one has failed" (Josh 23:14). For 110 years—far longer than most of us will live—Joshua watched the Lord, and he could say with confidence that the God they served was a promise keeper.

Well, sure, we might say. Joshua had it easy. He followed in Moses' footsteps and oversaw Israel when they were taking possession of their land. Giants notwithstanding, the hard part was over. But what about tough times? What then?

There was another leader of Israel who saw plenty of tough times. His best friend's father wanted to kill him in the worst way; his wife despised him for dancing a little too joyously; his children fought against each other and against him; he sinned against God and suffered greatly for his mistakes. This man, King David, had ample opportunity to put God to the test, yet he concluded, "The LORD is faithful to all his promises / and loving toward all he has made" (Ps 145:13); "Taste and see that the LORD is good; / blessed is the man who takes refuge in him" (Ps 34:8).

Through good times or bad, we can count on God. He has dealt with problems bigger than ours, and he has taken the time for problems smaller than ours. He will be there for us—he promises. Like the writer of Hebrews, "Let us hold unswervingly to the hope we profess, for he who promised is faithful" (Heb 10:23).

GOD DOES NOT LIE

Seth was out of college and working at his first job when he got a call from his mother telling him that his father had moved out.

His parents had fought occasionally through the years, but never anything serious enough to make Seth worried. Certainly he never imagined it would come to this. Seth hurried home and confronted his dad, who agreed it was all a mistake and decided to move back home. As Seth helped him unpack, his dad turned to him and said, "Don't worry, son. I won't do this again. I won't ever leave you again." A short time later, Seth's father moved out again, this time for good. Five years later, Seth says his father's lies are the major stumbling block in their relationship. He has caught his father in so many lies that trusting him seems impossible.

A person who says one thing and does another cannot be trusted. But we do not have to worry about that with God. If God says something, it is true, and he will abide by it. We can count on it. When God promises not to leave us, we can count on him being there. No matter how many times our parents have lied to us, misled us or let us down, we have a God who will always be faithful to us.

The writer of Hebrews makes it clear that truthfulness is an essential part of God's character: "Because God wanted to make the unchanging nature of his purpose very clear to the heirs of what was promised, he confirmed it with an oath. God did this so that, by two unchangeable things in which it is impossible for God to lie, we who have fled to take hold of the hope offered to us may be greatly encouraged. We have this hope as an anchor for the soul, firm and secure" (Heb 6:17-19). We can flee to a God who does not lie. We can run to him and fall into his arms! And we will find his embrace firm and secure.

These verses say not only that God does not lie but that it is impossible for him to do so. As one commentator pointed out, this is not a sign of God's weakness, mockingly suggested in the riddle "Can God make a rock so big he cannot lift it?" Rather, it is a sign of absolute strength and power.[9] The strength and power of his character are so great that they cannot be violated. That is why

Spurgeon called God's attributes "anchors to hold the soul from drifting in seasons of peril."[10] Part of God's character is absolute faithfulness.

1 Samuel 15:29 says, "He who is the Glory of Israel does not lie or change his mind; for he is not a man, that he should change his mind." As a woman, I lay claim to the feminine prerogative to change my mind. The cute shoes I had to have last season, I would not be caught dead in this season. I can repaint the living room in a weekend and "decide" on eight different ways to remodel my kitchen. That is fine for the little things in life, but it is not a trait we like in leaders, for obvious reasons. We like to know that the person in charge has thought through all the options and wisely chosen the best course to pursue, and we want to know that they are committed to that course of action. We criticize politicians who flip-flop on the issues, and we are demoralized when executives or church leaders begin something that promises to be the next greatest thing but then fail to follow through. When we catch our parents in a web of lies, we can feel like no one can be trusted.

We can rest in the knowledge that God does not change his mind. Otherwise, how could we rely on him for direction or be assured of his forgiveness—or trust anything he says? When God says he will do something, he will do it without wavering. The apostle Paul, after pronouncing a blessing on the Thessalonians, seals it by saying, "The one who calls you is faithful and he will do it" (1 Thess 5:24). It is a simple statement of absolute fact. Paul knew. He had faced as many trials as King David, if not more. He was imprisoned, stoned, shipwrecked and beaten (2 Cor 11:24-26). Yet, like David, Paul attested to the absolute faithfulness of the God he served, the same God we serve.

The years my dad did not speak to me hang like a cloud over our relationship. One of the few times I ever saw my grandpa get angry was over this issue. His own father had been present in body but distant in spirit, and he had determined to be different with his sons. He was quick to hug and kiss them and tell them how much he loved them. So it broke his heart to see his son cut off contact with me. Thankfully, Grandpa lived long enough to see the walls of silence come down. But for me, having experienced that kind of abandonment, the memory and possibility of it happening again tarnish my relationship with my dad. I am always too aware that he could disappear again just as easily as he once did.

I am so glad to know that God—my ever-present, loving, faithful God—will never disappear on me. He will never abandon me. He will never lie to me. He will never change his mind about his love for me. He has written my name on his palms and will never forget me.

Paul summed it up when he wrote, "God, who has called you into fellowship with his Son Jesus Christ our Lord, is faithful" (1 Cor 1:9). We can always count on God to come through for us because it his nature to be faithful. He cannot do otherwise. He will not let us down.

3

The Weight of the World

Y ou are so mature for your age." I heard those words a lot when I was growing up, from teachers, from relatives, from friends of my parents. Like many children of divorce, I possessed a maturity borne partly of personality and partly of necessity.

Since my mom had sole custody of me, I lived full time with her, and eventually with my stepfather and two brothers. This was my family, the people I lived with, the people who shaped my values, who tucked me into bed at night, who met with my teachers, who told me no when I wanted to go to unsupervised parties at a teenage friend's house. We were Christians of the conservative ilk, the kind of people who went to church whenever the doors were open. There was no picket fence, but we were close-knit and worked together pretty well.

But every summer I left this little cocoon and spent several weeks with Ponci and Grandpa, or occasionally with my dad. They were not bad people—far from it. But they had different values and different priorities from my family at home. For the two or three weeks I was with them, I knew that I would have the opportunity to do things my mom would never know about, things she would not approve of. The choice was mine.

The first day I arrived at my grandparents' house, they would take me to the grocery store to pick out snacks and breakfast foods. My cereal choices at home were limited to corn flakes, Grape-Nuts or plain Cheerios, so when given free rein to pick my own breakfast for the next two weeks, I worked hard to find the cereal with the most sugar, the brightest artificial color and the biggest load of dehydrated marshmallows all in one box. Choosing a nutritious cereal was a small test I failed every year, but there were bigger ones that mattered more.

The summer I was twelve, Ponci and Aunt Mart took me to the movies. We must not have decided what to see before we got there, because I remember standing in the lobby of the theater and looking at the movie posters. There was one movie about high schoolers in the 1950s that Ponci thought looked funny. The poster showed a woman's bare legs in a shower, with an eye peering through a hole in the wall of the shower stall. It was a comedy with the same name as a roly-poly cartoon character I knew well from watching hours of Looney Tunes on Saturday mornings. But *Porky's* the movie was rated R and did not look like anything Porky Pig and his Merrie Melodies pals would be acting in.

Ponci thought it looked fine, but I balked. I could not quite figure out what the movie was about, but the R rating was something I knew was off-limits. "I don't think my mother would want me to see that movie," I told her. I stood my ground, and we saw something rated PG instead. As it turned out, Mom was not too thrilled about me seeing *Poltergeist* either.

But this moral dilemma was one I had to face essentially alone. While my mom and stepdad could infuse me with Christian values and teaching for forty-nine or fifty weeks out of the year, there were two or three weeks each year that I was on my own, with people whose values were markedly different, when my faith and my convictions were put to the test. Fortunately they were small tests for the most part. A raunchy movie and a box of Count Chocula or Frankenberry cereal was about as bad as it got.

As I grew older, my faith and convictions solidified and became part of me, not just part of my family. I began to feel a growing divergence from my dad's family. I loved them dearly, but our paths were heading in different directions. I felt this most keenly when Ponci died.

The weekend I graduated from college, Ponci told me that she had Parkinson's disease. She'd had it for several years, and while she tired easily and stooped a little, she appeared pretty healthy. I didn't know much about the disease, except that she would shake a little and the shaking would get worse as the disease progressed. But eventually things got much worse. There came a day when she could not swallow, not even a sip of water, not even her own saliva. Ponci and Grandpa knew this day would come and had planned for it, deciding well beforehand that she would not get any feeding tubes or IVs. They wanted to let nature take its course.

My dad and uncle and I rushed to Illinois to be at Ponci's side during those final days. The morning she took her last breath, I was sleeping on a couch next to her hospital bed in the living room. Grandpa was resting in a recliner on her other side. He woke me after she was gone, and he told me that it was like she was not even there anymore. They had met as children, become high-school sweethearts and enjoyed more than fifty years of marriage together. He could sense that the woman who was still the love of his life was somehow gone in essence, even though her physical form lay right there in the bed. I nodded and told him, "Her spirit has left her body."

As we prepared for Ponci's funeral, I longed for the comfort that permeates a gathering of Christians at a funeral service, that sense of being in the midst of others who acknowledge and trust in God's sovereignty and grace. My great-grandma Fern was a devout Methodist but never really spoke openly about her faith, at least not to her family. As far as I could tell, she was the only other Christian believer in my dad's family. Standing before Ponci's open coffin, I felt more alone than I had ever felt in my life. I spent just a few weeks each year with my dad's family. The rest of the time I had just one home and one set of parents to please and obey. I did not have to constantly straddle the fence between the lives of two different families. I was fortunate.

The title of Elizabeth Marquardt's book on children of divorce, *Between Two Worlds*, reflects the impossible task of juggling two different families and somehow making sense of the whole mess. People talk about divorce as a split, but we kids are left straddling the chasm, trying precariously to balance each family while forging our own path through life. As Marquardt points out, when parents are married, together they take on the task of reconciling opposing views and values and deciding which direction the family is headed; all the kids have to do is go along for the ride. But when parents divorce, they no longer work together as a unit. They live separate lives, each in the way he or she pleases; then the kids must take on the job of reconciling these differences, making sense of competing worldviews. It is a tough job, and it takes a toll. We learn to be mature because we have to deal with mature issues and situations.

Adolescent psychologist Michael Bradley has seen the effects. In his book *Yes, Your Teen Is Crazy!* Bradley describes his frustration at the burden his young patients carry:

> I'm sorry, I truly am. I've tried and tried to maintain some semblance of the view that teenagers who experience the divorce of their parents can survive that process without trauma. I've tried to believe that these kids can be made to feel as healthy, secure, and positive about their futures as children from intact families. I've read those books about how teens can transfer their unfinished parenting needs to

a schedule of every other weekend and Wednesday evenings and be just fine.

It's not working. I may be burning out, but I've looked too often into confused and frightened adolescent eyes that stare blankly back at me when I try to sell them this view. Their eyes tell me what my stomach knows: It's just a lot of crap that we grownups use to rationalize our own failures to meet our commitments to our children. They know it.[1]

Phil, the second of four children, became the man of the house at the age of ten when his parents divorced and his older brother went to live with their dad. Their dad was already in a relationship and quickly remarried, while their mom remained single. Although Phil was still a young child, he felt responsible for and protective of his mom and younger siblings. At night he would lie awake listening to his mom crying in the next room, feeling helpless. When he and his siblings visited their dad, Phil would try to make sure they did not do family things that would hurt his mom's feelings, and when they did, he would try to keep the younger ones from talking about it when they got back home. When they did talk about such things, his mom, without meaning to, made them feel guilty for the fun they'd had. At his siblings' sporting events, when his mom and dad and stepmom were all present, Phil faced the dilemma of who to sit with. Unless they all sat together, Phil was sure to make someone unhappy. It was a no-win situation.

Phil is now married with children of his own. He says his years of trying to placate everyone have turned him into a peacemaker. Divorce experts Judith Wallerstein and Sandra Blakeslee describe in their book *What About the Kids?* the benefits of taking on adult-sized responsibility at a young age, like Phil had to do. In a chapter called "The Overburdened Child," they say that a child who does this well "learns compassion and how to take on a caregiving role.

She becomes a sensitive human being who is skilled at helping others. She also learns to be self-sufficient—a trait that will help her when she's an adult."[2]

Phil has learned these valuable skills because of the delicate balance he was forced to maintain between his parents. But at the same time, he dreads conflict and avoids it when possible. Phil would rather not bring up anything that bothers him because doing so makes him feel like there is something broken in the relationship. He would rather sweep it under the rug and pretend everything is fine, but he knows he cannot do that and have a healthy marriage. So he works hard to communicate well with his wife, even when it means dealing with conflicts, because he wants his marriage to work. He knows too well the heartache that divorce causes.

After all the growing-up years of balancing the needs of his mom and dad, the struggle is not over. When I talked to Phil, he was looking forward to seeing his dad over the weekend—but he was bracing himself for his mom's reaction when she learned of their visit.

Phil's situation is not unique. Many of us had to face complex adult issues with only a kid's limited life experience. We had to grow up quickly because adult problems were thrust on us.

Marquardt says children of divorce "wear a mantle of seriousness and vigilance even today that sets them apart from their peers. Childhood is about gradually maturing to become an adult who is able to think independently about complex moral issues. But children are not meant to take on this task alone."[3]

Whether we were meant for it or not, many of us were assigned that task and had to learn how to carry it out. Paul told the Corinthians, "When I became a man, I put childish ways behind me" (1 Cor 13:11). Children of divorce had to do that many years before becoming men and women. We had to put on the cloak of adulthood because the issues we were dealing with were adult issues.

Some of us faced financial difficulty when the primary breadwinner left, leaving the other parent to fend for the family alone. Some of us had to deal with a new stepfamily, sharing a room with a strange new sibling and figuring out what to call a new mom or dad. Some of us, like Phil, had to comfort parents or siblings while our own hearts were breaking in two. Some of us, like Lynn in the last chapter, had to find our own moral compass when our parents lost theirs. And many of us still have to juggle holidays and vacations between two sets of parents, not to mention in-laws. And if the in-laws are divorced, the problem is doubled!

Reading this list is sobering, isn't it? I feel weary just thinking about all the stress. I just want a break, a retreat, a safe place where things are simple, where Ozzie and Harriet stay married and we can all go home for Thanksgiving to eat turkey, play flag football and watch Macy's Thanksgiving Day Parade together. It sounds like heaven.

If our faith is in Christ, someday we will get there. In the meantime, we need some help here on earth. Fortunately, God does not make us wait until we reach the pearly gates to benefit from his promises. He is with us smack in the middle of all the messy situations we have to face in the here and now.

TOWER OF REFUGE AND STRENGTH

In the last chapter, we looked at God's faithfulness. God is always faithful in helping us; the Bible tells us that God is our help. A quick look at the names of God used in Scripture shows us a God who is on our side. There is *Jehovah Jireh,* "the God who will provide," and *Jehovah Nissi,* "the Lord our banner," a reference to the banner or flag that leads troops into battle. And there is the all-encompassing and soul-soothing *Jehovah Shammah,* "the Lord is there."

Sometimes that is all we need—to know that God is there. When we feel alone and adrift, hovering between two worlds or lost in a lonely country, it is good to know that God is there. He is there, in the midst of our pain, in the thick of our stress, in the middle of our messy situations. He is there when we need him.

Simply knowing that God is there would not mean much, however, if he were standing by ineffectually. What good does it do to be in God's presence if he is an impotent God? This question is addressed in the book *When Bad Things Happen to Good People*. The author, a rabbi, could not relinquish God's omniscience—his all-knowingness—but did relinquish God's omnipotence—his all-powerfulness. The author's conclusion was that God sees all the horrible things that happen in our lives, but he is powerless to stop them. Not much comfort there! Especially for children of divorce. If the rabbi is right, once again we are on our own, fighting our own battles, looking out for ourselves. God feels badly for us, but he cannot do anything about it.

Fortunately, the rabbi has it all wrong. This is not the picture that Scripture gives us. The Bible tells us that God is the Almighty. The psalms use the words "rock," "fortress," "tower"—words of strength and power.

Think about an epic movie with tremendous battle scenes. Countless hordes of the enemy army have set up camp, ready to storm in and overwhelm the smaller army. The enemies have spears and armor and snorting war horses. They are large and strong and brutish-looking, and they cover the ground like a swarm of ants.

But the smaller army has an advantage. They may be fewer in number and smaller in stature and not as mean in disposition. They may be brave and noble. But they would become legendary heroes who died in war if not for one thing—they are protected by the thick walls and high turrets of a fortress, a strong tower. Even the great hordes of soldiers amassed outside the gates cannot scale these walls, and their battering rams are no match for the solid entryways. That is the picture of God in Proverbs 18:10: "The name of the LORD is a strong tower; / the righteous run to it and are safe."

One of my favorite movies is *The Saint.* Val Kilmer plays Simon
Templar, a man of many disguises who steals things for the highest
bidder, until he falls for Emma Russell (played by Elisabeth Shue),
one of his targets. One scene always puts a lump in my throat. Simon and Emma are trapped in Moscow, a short distance from the
safety of the U.S. Embassy. With their enemies close by, however,
their chances of making it to the embassy seem slim. Simon creates a
distraction and sends Emma running toward the embassy. Despite
her head start, the main bad guy is just steps behind her and gaining
as she sprints toward the gates guarded by Marines.

As she nears the entrance, Emma yells, "I'm an American! I'm
an American! Open the gates!" The gates open and Emma falls ex-
haustedly into the arms of a strong soldier as another closes the gate
behind her. He tells the bad guy, "Back off from the gate. Back off!
I said, back off!" Emma's enemy glares menacingly at her, but he
cannot touch her. Now that she has made it into the safe haven of the
embassy, she is beyond the reach of her enemies.

That is the picture I get when I read Proverbs 18:10. "The name
of the LORD is a strong tower; / the righteous run to it and are
safe." I see a desperate, full-on sprint toward the last hope, the only
hope; a hope that, when reached, promises complete safety and an
end to the panicked run.

I must confess, however, that I am prone to stand and fight my
own battles when I should run to the high tower of God's protection.
We children of divorce are an independent bunch. We've traveled
alone on airplanes or trains, we've sometimes felt like outsiders in
our parents' homes, we've had to grow up fast and take care of ourselves. Independence becomes a habit that can be difficult to break.

I realized the foolishness of my independence when I had a
job that required me to travel frequently. I always packed light
when flying so I could travel with only carryon luggage, but at
just five feet two, I often had to stretch my height and my pitiful

arm muscles to hoist my carryon into and out of the overhead compartments. Men who were taller and stronger would offer to help, but I would say, "Thanks, I've got it." And I did manage it, but only with a fair amount of trouble. Finally, at the end of one long, exhausting day, I accepted an offer of help and watched while a gentleman lifted my carryon as if it were full of feathers and easily slid it into the storage bin. It was so easy for him, and he was so pleased to do it for me. I had refused help all those years, but no more. From then on, whenever a gentleman offered to help me stow my bag, I simply smiled, said thank you and stepped back to give him room.

We need to do that with God sometimes. He calls himself our help. He wants to help us in our trouble, but sometimes we are too independent or proud to accept his help. Instead we need to smile, say thank you and get out of the way.

SHARING THE BURDEN

The apostle Peter was not exactly known for his eloquence. He was a fisherman and is sometimes jokingly referred to as the disciple suffering from foot-in-mouth disease. Peter was passionate and opinionated, a combination that sometimes led him to make rash statements that prompted gentle rebukes from Jesus. After Pentecost, however, Peter was the first disciple to address the crowds gathered in Jerusalem, giving a stirring and beautiful speech about the reason for the exuberance and strange behavior of the Spirit-filled followers of Christ (Acts 2:14-39). Later Peter wrote two letters to the church, letters that have always drawn me in with their rich, literary feel. The fisherman's bumbling way of speaking was redeemed, and he became an eloquent defender of the faith and encourager of the faithful.

In Peter's first letter to the church, he acknowledged that these new believers faced difficult times. While things would later get much worse, those who professed Christ were already enduring bouts of mob violence that tested their faith and commitment. In the midst of this persecution, Peter encouraged them and told them, "Cast all your anxiety on him because he cares for you" (1 Pet 5:7). The believers reading Peter's letter had ample cause for anxiety. They did not have large churches or First Amendment protections. Scattered throughout the hostile Roman Empire, they felt like strangers and outsiders because of their faith. They needed to hear words of comfort, words reminding them that their God cared for them, that they did not have to carry the burdens of isolation and fear.

What burdens are you carrying? What anxieties weigh on you, leaving you feeling exhausted and weary? Many of us worry about our parents. How will they take care of themselves now that they are alone? Will they find love and marry again? Will we find love, and if we do, how will we make it last?

Like those early believers, we can take comfort in knowing that God cares about our burdens and that he is willing to help us with them. Psalm 68:19 says that God is "our Savior, / who daily bears our burdens." Not just once on a crowded plane or when things get desperate, but daily. Every single day, Jesus steps into the muddle of our lives, picks up our bag of troubles and lifts it to his shoulder. He wants to carry our burdens, if we will just let him. As the classic hymn says, "Are we weak and heavy laden, cumbered with a load of care? Precious Savior, still our refuge—Take it to the Lord in prayer!"

Jim had a hard time doing this. His parents never divorced, but his father had been distant and emotionally absent Jim's whole life, causing an ache Jim never really got over. Widowed and newly remarried, Jim found himself facing cancer. He feared that God was as distant and disinterested as his father had been. His wife had a strong faith and encouraged him to pray, but Jim would reply, "I don't want to bother God. He's got more important things to look after."

As Jim lay in a hospital bed in a critical-care unit, I talked with him about his reluctance to trust God. I assured him that God is able to provide all that we need, and he wants us to share our burdens with him. Jim was a father, so I reminded him that he would do anything to help his own children. I asked him to imagine how sad he would feel if one of his children needed something he could provide, but they were too proud to ask him for help or thought he would not care enough to help them. Jim nodded as he began to relate to a God who loves us as Jim loved his children, not as he had experienced his father's love. In a few minutes, Jim confessed his need for God's forgiveness and became a child of God. He died less than a week later. Jim was my paternal grandfather.

DÉJÀ VU ALL OVER AGAIN

It would be nice if our troubles ended when we reached adulthood, if the only difficulty we encountered from our parents' divorce entailed joint custody and summer visits. If only it were that simple. Instead, as Derrick described it to me, our parents' divorce can be like a death that never stops. Family therapist H. Norman Wright agrees: "When [a father] divorces or abandons the family it's worse than a death. . . . Of all the losses experienced in relationships, ambiguous loss is the most devastating kind because it is unclear. There is no certainty or closure about a person's absence or presence."[4]

Derrick has a good friend whose father died when they were both young. It was tragic and difficult; but, Derrick says, it happened once, and then it was over. By contrast, when Derrick's father left the family, he had to deal with the fallout over and over again, and it continues to this day.

When Derrick was about to turn forty, he was excited to hear that his dad would be traveling a long distance to be at his birthday party. It was a special affirmation to have his father coming. But Derrick's second thought was that it would be a difficult weekend because his mom would also be at the party; he would have to run interference between the two of them the whole time.

Derrick is not alone. Other children of divorce told me of family celebrations that were celebrated twice, once with each parent, or that required careful orchestration of events so one parent would be leaving before the other arrived. In the mid-1990s, the sitcom *Friends* aired an episode about a birthday party for Rachel Green, played by Jennifer Aniston, whose parents were divorced. At the party, Monica and Phoebe kept Rachel's mother busy at one apartment while across the hall Chandler and Joey kept Rachel's father entertained at an identical party. While it makes for humorous sitcom material, parents who cannot attend a family gathering without fighting make for lousy company.

If only we could control our parents in these situations, somehow make them behave by the force of our will. Things would be so much easier if they could just get along. But for some of us, seeing our parents get along peacefully is a dream that will never materialize. The acrimony and bitterness they have toward one another makes every meeting a potential powder keg. When we are faced with a situation like that, all we can do is pray that God will give us grace and strength to get through the times of strife, and wisdom to navigate between our parents.

The prophets did more than warn the Israelites of the doom and gloom that would befall them if they did not repent and serve God. They also provided encouragement to God's people in exile. Far away from their home, with little hope of returning in their lifetime, living as slaves and captives—they needed strength to endure.

God had some beautiful things to say to the captive Israelites through the prophet Isaiah:

When you pass through the waters,
  I will be with you;

and when you pass through the rivers,
    they will not sweep over you.
When you walk through the fire,
    you will not be burned;
    the flames will not set you ablaze.
For I am the LORD, your God,
    the Holy One of Israel, your Savior;
I give Egypt for your ransom,
    Cush and Seba in your stead.
Since you are precious and honored in my sight,
    and because I love you,
I will give men in exchange for you,
    and people in exchange for your life. (Is 43:2-4)

Although written for a specific people at a specific time, these verses are still true expressions of the character of God and the nature of our struggles on earth. As we go through life, whether we trust in God or not, we will walk through some deep waters. Certainly our parents' divorce was a patch of deep water that threatened to drown us. Others will come. There will be tough times when we feel the heat of flames, or the strong current of a river around our neck. God does not promise that we will live trouble-free lives. But he does promise that we will not be overcome by the trials that come our way, and that he will be right there with us through every ordeal.

The year that Ponci died was one of the hardest years of my life. It began when my family came to stay with me for a few weeks, and through a series of circumstances they wound up staying for a year. I went from living alone to sharing a small townhouse with two other adults, two teenage boys and a large dog. I was dealing with a stressful job situation, and then I lost my job. So I no longer had that stress, but I also no longer had a paycheck. Three months after that, I got the call that Ponci was dying. A few weeks after Ponci died, my mom was diagnosed with cancer. I began to take Tums like candy as my body turned the stress into stomach acid. I was up to my neck in the current, but the waters did not sweep over me. My anchor during this time was a weekly Bible-study group that met at a friend's house. They prayed for me and my family during this rough year, and they supported us in practical ways, knowing that we would repay the kindness when the situations were reversed.

The end of the passage in Isaiah is something we need to remember: "Since you are precious and honored in my sight, / and because I love you, / I will give men in exchange for you." How can we not run to a God like that? The passion he has for us means that he will do anything for us. And in fact he gave the life of a man, his own Son, Jesus Christ, for us. That is how much he loves us!

A SURE PATH

Negotiating the territory between our parents can be a dangerous mission. There are land mines of accusation and guilt to avoid; there is shrapnel from hurt feelings and the mortar rounds of bitterness to watch out for. And should our mission fail, we could be facing all-out war. Little wonder that we sometimes find ourselves tiptoeing tentatively through the twists and turns of our parents' worlds. The way is uncertain and the outcome could be ugly.

To navigate the battlefields that our parents' divorce may have established, we need a guide. We need someone who has been along this path, who has marked all the land mines and knows where the snipers hide. We need a guide who knows the route well and can confidently take us safely through it unharmed.

One of my favorite verses is from Isaiah: "Whether you turn to the right or to the left, your ears will hear a voice behind you, saying, 'This is the way; walk in it'" (30:21). I don't know about you, but it is comforting to me to know that God guides our steps and that he will always let us know which way we should be going. Notice, however, that Isaiah says the voice is behind us and we will not hear it until we are making a turn. We want to see the whole route marked out, but that is not how God guides us. He does not give us a map and send us on our independent way. Instead, he is with us each step of the way, telling us which way to go, confirming our path and encouraging us to keep going.

We carry a heavy burden as children of divorce, and while that burden can strengthen us, it can also crush us under its weight. When our backs are bowed low and our steps falter, God is there to relieve us. Trying to carry all the burdens thrust on us by our parents' divorce is an exercise in futility and frustration. God does not expect us to deal with it alone or to just buck up. He wants us to lean on him and let him lighten our load. All we have to do is let go.

4

All You Need Is Love

I did it at both my high school and college graduations. It was silly, I know. He was not going to be there. He probably did not even know what day graduation was, and he had not spoken to me in several years. Still, as I stood with my classmates, walked to the elevated platform for my diploma and returned to my seat, I scanned the crowd, hoping to catch a glimpse of him. I did not expect him to be front and center, but I thought maybe he would be on the outskirts, leaning against the fence or peering around a doorway.

I was looking for my dad, of course. I did not expect to see him, but I hoped he would show up. I imagined that our eyes would meet and he would smile at me. I would wave excitedly, and he would nod his head with pride before turning around and leaving quietly. Just a glimpse. That was all I wanted.

I never told anyone about that secret hope. Then when I was in my twenties, a friend of mine told me about her friend Becky, whose parents were divorced. Becky's father had left and started a new family with his new wife, cutting off contact with his first wife and kids. Becky tracked down her missing-in-action father and showed him photos of all the things he had missed: her birthdays, her first boyfriend, her prom. She told him that she had looked for him at her high school and college graduations, hoping to see him even if he only waved and disappeared.

I nearly choked when I heard this story and tears filled my eyes. It had never occurred to me that I was not the only one with that secret longing, the hidden hope that a father who appeared to not care would prove me wrong by just showing up.

Many of us whose parents divorced lost a mother or a father. All of the advice books for parents who are divorcing tell them to reassure their children that the divorce is all about Mom and Dad, not about the kids. But let's face it: sometimes a divorce is about running away, not just from the deserted spouse but from everything and everyone. Sometimes it is about no longer wanting to be a father or a mother just as much as no longer wanting to be a husband or wife. Sometimes we kids truly are left behind and divorced in just as real a way as the remaining spouse.

Tamara Tanner's father, Roscoe, was a high-profile tennis player in the 1970s. His exciting Wimbledon championship match against favorite Bjorn Borg was the first live "Breakfast at Wimbledon" broadcast on American television and convinced network executives that Americans would get up early on a Saturday morning to watch a tennis match in England. Tamara grew up being close to her father, but he was on a downward spiral of gambling, infidelity and drugs that eventually landed him in prison. In the midst of all this, he deserted his family, leaving his daughter Tamara to wonder, *How could he really love me and not come home? He pretty much erased us from his life. I didn't think that was humanly possible.*[1]

Even if our parents truly love us, sometimes the physical distance meant they missed milestones in our lives, along with everyday routines and experiences that shaped us and made us who we are today. I remember being a little put out when my dad made a joke about my high school class ring. The school name had been too long, so "Regional" had been abbreviated as "Reg." My dad had said, laughing, "What's this? 'Regular' school?" Normally I love his sense of humor, but it stung me to realize that he did not even know the name of my school. It was a little thing, but another reminder of how divergent our lives were becoming as I got older and Dad missed more and more of my life.

As humans, we were created with an innate need for love. It is part of God's way of drawing us to himself. He alone is the source and definition of love, and he has built into us a desire for the very thing that he is. For many of us, life is one long struggle to find love. We desperately want our parents to love us, and later, our spouses and children. We want to be loved in the workplace and the community. We crave the pleasure and contentment that comes from knowing that others esteem us.

When that desire for love is frustrated at an early age, we can begin to doubt whether we are capable of being loved. "Maybe it's me," we think. "Maybe something in me is broken." Or we worry that we are not up to the task of loving others well. That was Derrick's worry. He has been married for ten years now and is a loving father and husband. His wife, who was present when I interviewed him, thinks he is a great husband; but even after a decade of marriage, he worries that he does not have what it takes to be a good spouse.

Then there is John. Since his parents' marriage fell apart, he finds it impossible to trust. He does not know how to relate to women, he tells me, laughing because his leg is shaking as he tells me about a woman who has touched his heart. His inability to trust gets in the way of his heart, though; he sees lies and infidelity where he knows there are none. He does not want to get married. But then he reads to me from his journal, where he writes about a future wife and family. There is hope buried inside, but he is afraid to follow it. In his journal, John writes of his fear that his wife would leave him, that they would not be able to understand each other, to communicate well, to love well. He expresses fear of being tempted to infidelity, a temptation that could be controlled but not eliminated. What if he were the one to cause his own marriage to fail?

Nathan was nineteen when his parents divorced, but their relationship had been rocky long before the legal documents were filed. They were waiting for the kids to leave home before ending the marriage, but that hardly stopped the divorce from having a big impact on their children. Now thirty-seven, Nathan has only recently acknowledged the depths to which his parents' divorce has affected him, particularly in his relationships with women. Throughout his twenties and early thirties, Nathan continually dated and broke up with women, which seemed normal at the time. But as he nears forty, he has begun to realize that there is something broken about the way he approaches romantic relationships. Until recently, he believed arguing always led down the path to divorce, so whenever he and a girlfriend would have a disagreement, he figured the relationship was doomed to failure, and he would end it. The pressure on Nathan to have a successful marriage is doubly high. Not only does he know that God hates divorce, but he is also a pastor at a growing church and knows that a failed marriage could cost him his career and calling.

In *The Unexpected Legacy of Divorce*, Judith Wallerstein tells of two young women, one whose parents were still married and who was happily married herself, the other whose parents were divorced and who remained unmarried. As Wallerstein talked with the two women, she discovered that the difference between them was subtle but significant. The woman from the intact family never questioned that she would one day meet the man of her dreams and live happily ever after. She assumed the fairy tale would come true for her. The girl from the broken home did not hold the same assumption. For her, the fairy tale bore no relation to her expectations of real life.

Sadly, no one else seems to expect the fairy tale to come true for us either. We are told dire statistics of how much more likely we are to be divorced ourselves or to never marry. As a single woman, I have met my share of men who decided that my parents' divorce was reason enough to reject me. It did not seem to matter to them that my mom and stepfather have been married more than thirty years. They saw me as tainted by the failure of the first marriage and branded me as too risky. Not every prospective beau thinks that way, but it has happened more often than I would have thought plausible.

An article appearing on a reputable Christian website reinforces this "divorce kid" phobia, saying we are "maimed for love and intimacy," lack any "successful models," and are "not good bets for promise keeping."[2] Whatever happened to the notion of a God who redeems and transforms us?

In the movie *Sleepless in Seattle*, one of my favorite lines comes from Rosie O'Donnell's character: "You don't want to be in love; you want to be in love in a movie." It's true. I want to be in love in a movie. Movies are a lot neater than real life. Boy meets girl, impossible situations ensue, but you know that in the end boy and girl will get together and live happily ever after. Everything gets tied up in a nice, neat bow. And it all happens in the space of about two hours. With movie love, I know what happens, and it happens quick.

We do not get the same luxury in real life. Things are messy, sometimes really messy. Neat bows have a way of getting crushed or coming untied. The ending is never entirely certain. Will the boy get the girl? Will the girl even meet the boy? Will the fairy tale fall apart in divorce, death, dullness?

TO KNOW ME IS TO LOVE ME

In order to really love someone, we have to know them well. We know this to be true of romantic love. Learning all about another person is one of the joys of budding romance. My idea of a good first date is that the evening ends only when the restaurant employees are sweeping the floors and putting chairs on tables around you. You spend hours just talking because there is so much to learn. And every bit as thrilling as learning all about the other person is having them learn all about you. Where did that scar come from, who did you go with to your high school prom, what one thing have you always dreamed about? At our deepest level, we want to be known.

Parental love is no different. We need our parents to understand us, to accept us for who we are, to love us. And loving someone requires knowing them. This principle works both ways. Sometimes we need to know our parents in a way that we have never known them before.

Nathan always blamed his father for the breakup of his parents' marriage. His mother had always complained about his father, and his father had never defended himself against her accusations. When Nathan was in his mid-thirties, he became frustrated by the shortcomings he saw in his own approach to relationships and asked his father to tell him the whole story behind the divorce. What he learned radically changed his opinion of his father. During Nathan's teen years, his mother had an ongoing, adulterous affair. Nathan was given his father's journals, which told the story of a husband who loved an adulterous wife and tried unsuccessfully to win back her love over a period of years. Learning this truth about his parents' divorce gave Nathan a tremendous, newfound respect for his father.

Not all of us are going to learn such life-altering truths about our parents. And some of us are never going to have parents who will take the time to really learn who we are. Our parents are not perfect—but God is, and he loves us perfectly at all times. In fact the Bible tells us that "God is love" (1 Jn 4:16). He is the perfect embodiment of everything love is. One commentary puts it this way:

> To comprehend the sweeping character of the statement *God is love*, substitute the name of anyone you know—your mother, pastor, friend, a well-known Christian or hero of the faith or even yourself—for "God." Few are the people we would describe simply with the word love. Mom may be the most loving person you have known. She may have shown you what mature, self-giving, genuine love is like. But no matter how full, rich and steadfast her love, the statement "Mom is loving," can never be changed into "Mom is love." For love does not characterize her as it characterizes God.[3]

To know what love is, all we have to do is look at God. Bill Hybels writes, "God passionately yearns to be in a loving relationship with the people He created."[4] A lot of people think of God as some big ghost in the sky who may have gotten the universe started but who is not involved in what we do every day. The truth is that God is very interested in and involved in our daily activities because he loves us and he longs for us to love him too.

WE LOVE BECAUSE HE FIRST LOVED US

Years ago I heard Joshua Harris give a devotional talk on knowing God. Josh is senior pastor of Covenant Life Church in Gaithersburg, Maryland, and the author of several books. A newlywed at the time, Josh used a fictional illustration from marriage to demonstrate how God wants us to love him.

Josh asked the audience to imagine that he was coming home to his wife, Shannon, at the end of a long workday. All he wanted to do was to feel her love and just be with her. Shannon blushed and appreciated his adoring gaze. Then she tried to tell him of her day, but he kept shushing her again and again so he could just enjoy the quiet and tell her how much he loved her. He asked the audience to imagine Shannon's frustration over wanting to tell her new husband about her day, wanting him to share in the experience, feeling like many young lovers that an experience was not truly real until she told him about it—but having her dearest shush her over and over. Then he asked us to imagine how God feels when we want to experience the emotional intimacy of God's presence without taking the time and trouble to study God and get to know who he is.

In the imaginary scenario, Shannon was happy to be with her husband, but she was not content with his mere presence. She wanted to know everything about him, and she wanted him to know everything about her, down to the little details of how she spent her day while he was at work.

When we take the time to study God, to learn about him through his Word and through the words of others who know him and through prayer, he is pleased. Like a bridegroom, he is delighted that we desire to know as much as we can about him.

As vitally important as it is for us to know God, it is also important to know that God knows us. He "gets" us. He knows what makes us tick, what makes us laugh, what makes us cry. He knows our favorite color and our favorite flavor of ice cream. He remembers our birthdays and knows how many freckles are on our noses. He sees that gray hair we try to hide, and he remembers how we got every scar on our bodies. No one will ever know us as well as the One who made us.

David knew this, and he expressed it beautifully in Psalm 139: "O LORD, you have searched me / and you know me. / You know when I sit and when I rise; / you perceive my thoughts from afar. / You discern my going out and my lying down; / you are familiar with all my ways. / Before a word is on my tongue / you know it completely, O LORD" (vv. 1-4).

Well of course, we might say. God is omniscient, that is, he knows everything. But as Matthew Henry points out in his commentary, the psalmist does not say, "'Thou hast known *all*,' but, 'Thou hast known *me*.'"[5] This is the same God who rules the stars, who laid out the foundations of the earth, who controls the weather and provides food for the wild animals. He has a lot on his mind, but he also has us on his mind. Psalm 139 says he pays such close attention to us that he knows when we sit down or get up, when we go to bed and when we go out for a while. He knows everything there is to know about us, including, I would venture to say, a few things we do not even know about ourselves. To be known in this intimate way is a sure sign of God's love for us.

Stop and think for a moment about how God shows his love for you as an individual. Take a piece of paper and write down all the things—big and small—God does to show you his love. Now tuck that list away in a safe place. The next time you wonder if anyone loves you or what exactly love is or whether God is for real, you can pull out that list and remind yourself of the greatest love you will ever know.

Therapists tell us to learn to love ourselves, and Whitney Houston sang that this was "the greatest love." But the greatest love is not the love I have for myself; it is the love God has for me. For years Dawn Eden, author of *The Thrill of the Chaste*, bought into the idea that she needed to love herself. It was what all the self-help books and magazines assured her was most important. But then one day she realized that loving herself was not enough. "It's not hard," she wrote, "for me to find someone to love the me I love. What I never imagined before I was chaste was that I could hope to find someone to love the me I don't love."[6]

Many of us are terrified of being known intimately. We know the ugly parts of our souls, the parts we do not love. We are afraid that it is only a matter of time before the truth comes out, the ugliness is exposed and we are left alone and rejected.

The good news about God is that he has already seen every ugly corner of our dark souls. None of it surprises him; none of it has been kept secret from him. He knows it all and loves us anyway.

Our loving bridegroom says, "Though the mountains be shaken / and the hills be removed, / yet my unfailing love for you will not be shaken" (Is 54:10). Speaking of this verse, eighteenth-century Baptist preacher John Gill wrote:

> The love of God to his people is an everlasting love; it always continues; it never did, nor never will depart, notwithstanding their fall in Adam, their depraved state by nature, their actual sins and transgressions, their many revoltings and backslidings; though the Lord may hide his face from them, and afflict them, still he loves them; whatever departs from them, his kindness shall not; though riches may flee away from them, friends stand aloof off from them, health may be taken away, and life itself, yet the love of God is always the same.[7]

This is a love we can cling to. This is a love that will not fade when we are no longer a chick magnet or when a new spouse and stepkids come along. There is nothing we can do to lose God's love, and there is nothing we can do to make God love us more, because he already loves us perfectly and completely.

You may be asking, then why did God let this happen? Why did God let my parents grow apart and divorce? Why did he not heal their marriage, rekindle their love, keep us all together?

People have pondered the source and meaning of suffering for years. The age-old question of how a loving God can allow terrible things to happen always seems to haunt us. Archibald MacLeish's Pulitzer Prize–winning play *J.B.*, a secular retelling of the story of Job, carries this piercing refrain: "If God is God, He is not good; if God is good, He is not God."[8] As children of divorce, we have known our own brand of suffering. We may be tempted to think, like MacLeish, that God must either be unable or unwilling to alter our state. But he is neither. Psalm 62:11-12 says, "One thing God has spoken, / two things have I heard: / that you, O God, are strong, / and that you, O Lord, are loving."

There is a perfect balance in these verses and in God's divine character. He is not a lopsided God, ineffectually caring for us or unwittingly crushing us with his enormous power. Instead, he is a God of perfect harmony, seamlessly blending strength and love.

What a tremendous comfort! God is both strong enough to handle anything that comes our way, and he is loving enough to care. He is God (all-powerful), and he is good (all-loving).

FICKLE LOVE
Some of us grew up in families where one of our parents had primary custody and the other had visitation rights. We may have felt the love of our noncustodial parent wane as time and distance separated us. We may wonder if God's love for us will fade as well. Can we get too far away for God to love us?

Paul assured us that this is not possible. In his letter to the Romans he writes, "I am convinced that neither death nor life, neither angels nor demons, neither the present nor the future, nor any powers, neither height nor depth, nor anything else in all creation, will be able to separate us from the love of God that is in Christ Jesus our Lord" (Rom 8:38-39). Notice the word Paul uses—*convinced*. This was a man who had experienced incredible trials and would go on to experience even more. He was beaten, run out of town, slandered, imprisoned and stoned. Yet he was absolutely certain—*convinced*—of the enduring and unfailing love of God.

John Piper preached on this text right after September 11, 2001. Piper has spent years teaching that we derive our greatest pleasure in God and in bringing him glory. His rallying cry on that bleak day after the terrorist attacks was the unshakable love of our Savior. "What is our hope in the best and worst of times? When all around our soul gives way? Our hope is that nothing can separate us from the love of God in Christ, not even suffering and death. Our hope is not for an easy or comfortable or secure life on this earth. Our hope is that the love of God will grant us joy in the all-satisfying glory of God which will continue through death and increase for all eternity."[9]

LIVING IN HOPE

I grew up around water. If there was a place to swim within a few hours' drive of wherever we lived, we found it. We lived in an apartment complex for two summers and had a pool right outside our back door, but usually our swimming holes were of the old-fashioned variety, the kind that are murky and full of fish. I love to swim and learned to do so at a young age. My brothers learned even younger. By the time they were born, my family lived in New Jersey, near our grandparents who owned a small summer cottage on a lake. My kid brothers were bobbing on the waves with the rest of us when they could barely walk.

We did not just learn to swim, though. We learned to respect the water. We were lectured on the necessity of checking out unfamiliar areas carefully before jumping or diving into the water. We were lectured on the dangers of drinking alcohol around water long before we reached the legal drinking age. During the few winters that were cold enough to freeze the lake, we got to ice skate and ice fish—after we heard lectures about not walking on cracked ice or ice bubbles, and what to do if someone fell through the ice.

We loved the water. We spent hours swimming, floating and boating. We dove with abandon off the dock at our grandparents' place, having long ago located all the dangers below the surface.

But if we ever swam somewhere else, even next door, we would only dive off the dock when cousins or siblings were standing on the rocks to clearly mark them. We were well aware of the serious danger that water can pose to anyone who does not respect it or who treats it cavalierly or who is so afraid of it that they never learn to swim.

That is how I feel about marriage. I would love to experience it, to swim and float in the pure delight of a husband's love, to discover what lies beneath the murky depths of a man's mind, even sometimes to wrinkle my nose in surprised disgust at the toe-grabbing seaweed of a man's less refined habits.

But I know marriage is not a thing to be entered into lightly. It is a solemn vow and commitment before God. It is also something that requires work. I did not learn to swim in a day, and even after I learned, there was a process of becoming more proficient and then of learning new strokes. And there were times of stretching: gaining the confidence to swim out to the float; being in awe of Grandpa, who could swim across the whole lake; taking aquatic aerobics in college, which turned out to be a grueling class of swimming laps.

A friend of mine who is married got some concerned looks when she was seen with a book with the subtitle *Building an Affair-Proof Marriage*. Was her marriage in trouble? No, but she knows that danger always lurks (1 Pet 5:8), and she was taking no chance of it catching her unaware. I think she is a wise woman.

Phil is one of the seemingly successful children of divorce that Elizabeth Marquardt describes in *Between Two Worlds*. Phil shared with me the heartache and difficulty of his family situation, but I also know him to be a loving husband and father. When I asked him about his marriage, he told me that he works hard at it. He is committed to doing whatever it takes to make his marriage work. He knows that God hates divorce, and he has seen firsthand the devastation that divorce causes the children and couple involved. Phil does not want his three daughters to have to go through what he did.

Phil does not remember his parents arguing. In fact, he does not remember much about his childhood, which he attributes to the fact that it was basically good and untroubled. Looking back, he thinks his parents simply did not deal with the problems that arose in their marriage. They were only concerned with maintaining an appearance that everything was fine. Then it all fell apart.

Like his parents, Phil would rather not deal with conflict. To him, talking to his wife about issues either of them has with the other feels like admitting failure. But he knows how important communication is in a good marriage, so instead of glossing over conflicts, Phil talks them over with his wife. No matter how uncomfortable it is, he knows that dealing with conflict is vitally important to the health of his relationship with his wife.

Phil's great marriage is no accident or anomaly. It is the result of hard work and the grace of God. Our holy Father's love for us is so great that he is willing to redeem us from the most difficult circumstances, and he is strong enough to make that happen.

CHILDREN OF GOD

John was known as the disciple whom Jesus loved. As far as we know, it was not other people who called him that; he gave himself that moniker. Was he trying to play favorites, to insist that Jesus liked him better than the other eleven guys in his inner circle? No. John was reveling in the joyous, awesome knowledge that he—John, the youngest disciple, one of a pair of brothers Jesus nicknamed "sons of thunder"—was loved by the Messiah. John understood that the love Jesus had for him was the same love that the Father in heaven had for him. Inspired by the Holy Spirit, he penned these words: "How great is the love the Father has lavished on us, that we should be called children of God! And that is what we are!" (1 Jn 3:1).

Notice the word John uses for this love. God does not parse it out or grudgingly sprinkle it on us. He *lavishes* it on us. When I read that word, I think of a huge hotel room with satin sheets on the bed and heavy draperies on the windows, with every surface covered in fresh flowers and loaded shopping bags, and me reclining in a giant, bubble-filled tub with strawberries and champagne nearby. *Lavish* is more than I could ever hope for or expect. It is over the top, extravagant. The dictionary uses the words "profuse" and "excess" to describe the meaning of *lavish*, which likely comes from a Middle French word meaning "to pour down."

The King James Version of 1 John 3:1 says, "Behold, what manner of love"—as in, what kind of love is this? From where did it originate? We have not seen anything like this before!

The world and the naysayers would call us *children of divorce*. They would define us by this one event, this one failure, of which we were merely bystanders caught in the crossfire. Our circumstances, in the minds of some, become our destiny. But God has a different view of us. He does not call us children of divorce; he calls us his very own children.

We do not deserve to be called God's children. It is a lavish grace, lovingly bestowed. In the kingdom of heaven, we are not the poor beggars at the gates or the scullery maids sweeping the ashes out of the kitchen grates. We are the children, seated at the banquet table, wearing fine clothes, set to inherit the kingdom. Not because of anything we have done, but because we have a Father in heaven who is everything we have ever dreamed of, everything we have ever needed.

Do not underestimate the love God has for you. Do not limit him by the experience and understanding of love you've received through the imperfections of your parents. Let him love you in the way that only he can. I pray for you, as Paul prayed for the

Christians in Ephesus, "that you, being rooted and established in love, may have power, together with all the saints, to grasp how wide and long and high and deep is the love of Christ" (Eph 3:17-18).

Our Father's love is yet another way that he is faithful to us. We can count on his love at all times, in all circumstances, regardless of how we feel or how things look. God loves us without hesitation, no holds barred. "And so we know and rely on the love God has for us. God is love" (1 Jn 4:16).

5

Things That Go
Bump in the Night

Soon after my mom and dad divorced, I began having violent
nightmares. I remember waking up screaming, sitting up in my bed,
all the covers tangled in a heap on the floor. My mother would be
there to comfort and calm me and get me back to sleep, but the memory of the nightmares lingered. To this day, I can recall at least one
of those nightmares in vivid detail, and it is an experience I never
want to have again. Back then there were no handy reference guides
to "your child after the divorce," but Mom faithfully recorded my
nightmare stage in my baby book, along with my first haircut and
favorite toddler toys. She was wise enough to realize that these scary
dreams were part of the aftermath of divorce in my life.

The violent nightmares ended, but throughout my childhood
I harbored a secret fear that violence would befall my family. While
other kids were afraid of the dark or scared of the bogeyman, I
remember being terrified that someone would break into our house
at night and murder all of us—with either an ax or a chain saw. I
would not sleep without at least a sheet covering me, to provide
a little protection. (If the fear was irrational, the solution could

be too!) I would devise escape plans, and plot how I would alert and rescue the other members of my family and think about where I would hide.

The truth is, I still have this fear. If I hear an odd noise at night, my first thought is that someone has broken into the house. From my bed, I think about whether I should hide in the closet or make a run for the front door. How quickly can I dial 911? What objects in my bedroom can I use as weapons? Should I grab the car keys so I can drive off, or should I run to a neighbor's house and begin pounding on the door?

My mom has a similar fear of fires. In hotels, she always looks for the exits and knows where the fire extinguishers are. At home, she thinks about how she would get everyone out of the house, and she is relieved that we are all adults now and can fend for ourselves. When my brothers were little and we lived in the city, our bedroom windows were just a few feet away from the house next to ours. Mom told me once about her escape plan for that house: if a fire broke out, she would climb out the boys' window, wedge her back against one house and her feet against the other, and shimmy down to the ground with both boys on her lap. I assured her I would shimmy over from my bedroom window and take one of the boys down with me.

My mom knows why she has this fear. When she was a child, an insurance salesman came to her parents' house and showed them a film of houses burning down. I don't know whether Grandma and Grandpa bought fire insurance that day, but the images my mom saw left her with a lifelong fear of being caught in a fire.

My fear was different. It seemed to come from nowhere. I always had an early bedtime, and other than seeing *Poltergeist* that one time, I was never allowed to watch scary movies. No one had ever broken into our house or the houses of anyone we knew.

The origin of my irrational fear eluded me. But Judith Wallerstein and Sandra Blakeslee state that the fear of strangers breaking into

the home is not uncommon among children of divorced parents.[1]
Researcher Dr. Neil Kalter observed this fear in two separate children in his clinical work.[2] Linda Jacobs, author of the Divorce-
Care for Kids curriculum, told me her son had similar fears after
her divorce, and Elizabeth Marquardt wrote that as a child she
"imagined strangers peeping in our windows or looking through
the skylight of my attic bedroom."[3] In fact, Marquardt found
that those of us from divorced homes felt significantly less safe—
emotionally and physically—when we were growing up than our
peers from intact families.[4]

While some of us did live in unsafe situations after our parents'
divorce—bad neighborhoods, a string of questionable adults coming through our lives and homes, a violent stepparent or depressed
parent—many of us lived in relative safety. Our fears were often
rooted in the loss of a male presence in our homes. Dads are the
ones who are supposed to go downstairs with the baseball bat to
investigate strange noises in the middle of the night. They are the
tall, strong ones whose job it is to protect the family from outside
forces. Having divorced parents when we were growing up, however, usually meant living with our mother and visiting our father
only on weekends or holidays or summer vacations. Without a
father in the house, we felt vulnerable and unprotected. For me at
least, that feeling did not go away even after my mom remarried
and we had a strong man in the house to protect us. That early
vulnerability was already deeply ingrained.

Childhood is a magical time of life when we are sheltered in the
nest of our families. As I walked around my neighborhood earlier
this week, I saw a young bird sitting beneath a tree and chirping
for all it was worth. Either he had fallen out of his nest or mama
bird had kicked him out in an effort to teach the little tyke to fly.
In either case, he was alone in an unfamiliar place and obviously
scared. His frantic little chirp was a clear plea for help.

Like that little bird, some of us have felt alone and terrified and vulnerable in a hostile world full of blue jays and neighborhood cats. Whether it was our mom or dad who was absent, we felt the void in our lives. We missed having someone to give us advice, lock the doors at night, make us eat our vegetables and do all the other things that parents were supposed to do to look out for us.

The protective role our parents play in our lives evolves as we grow older. Instead of tucking us into bed at night and making sure we wash behind our ears, they ask probing questions of our dates, show us how to file our taxes and take us shopping for our first business suit. Without them, we feel lost even as we learn to navigate the world in our own way. Marquardt describes it as a "sense of having to figure out everything in life alone, expecting no help from anyone else."[5]

Debbie was raised by her mother and her mother's second husband, who adopted her after Debbie's father disappeared when she was three. Although her parents were not Christians, they sent Debbie to a local Christian school because it offered a better-quality education than the public school. Debbie gave her life to Christ and after high school chose to attend a Christian college. But while Debbie was trying to live out her faith, her parents decided to go their separate ways. They divorced while Debbie was in high school. The only real dad she had ever known was gone, and Debbie had never had a close relationship with her mother. She felt very alone in the world.

At college, still reeling from her parents' divorce, Debbie found acceptance with the party crowd, and in her own words "went a little wild." The party ended quickly however, when Debbie discovered she was pregnant. She and her boyfriend broke up, and Debbie was left to pick up the pieces and begin life as a single mother. When she first learned she was pregnant, Debbie remembers feeling a deep sadness, thinking particularly of how disappointed her adopted father would have been—if he had known. But he was gone from her life.

Eleven years later, Debbie finds herself repeating her past. She is pregnant again, and still a single mother. Her second child's father wants to be involved in the baby's life but is no longer interested in marriage. Debbie told me she cannot believe she let this happen to her once, let alone twice. She feels certain that her life would not have turned out this way if she had had a father around, someone to hold her accountable, someone to talk with in a way she could not talk with her mother, someone to give her a man's perspective on the men she was dating.

She is probably right. Pediatrician Meg Meeker writes in her excellent book *Strong Fathers, Strong Daughters,* "Divorce is really the central problem that has created a generation of young adults who are at higher risk for chaotic relationships, sexually transmitted diseases, and confusion about life's purpose."[6] Particularly in cases like Debbie's, where one parent's role essentially ends when the marriage ends, we children are left with a truncated perspective on relationships, life and our very selves.

OUR FATHER WHO ART IN HEAVEN

The whole concept of fatherhood was initiated by God to teach us something about his special relationship with us, his children. God calls himself our Father throughout Scripture, particularly in the New Testament. Jesus had an earthly father, Joseph, who was a stepfather of sorts. But after Jesus' early years, we hear nothing about this influential man. Presumably Joseph died before Jesus began his ministry, since at the cross Jesus asked his friend John to take care of his mother, Mary. John tells us that Mary went to live with him and remained with him for the rest of her life (Jn 19:26-27), so it is probable that Joseph had died, leaving Mary a widow in need of a son to provide for her in her old age.

Although we do not read much about Joseph in the Bible, we see Jesus frequently taking time to check in with his Father in heaven. In times of stress or weariness, or in preparation for upcoming events sure to drain his energy and emotion, Jesus retreated from his hordes of followers and found a quiet place to pray to God. There, on a mountaintop or in a garden, Jesus told the Father the things that troubled him. He asked for strength to complete the tasks assigned to him, and he reminded himself of the Father's faithfulness and love toward his beloved Son.

The disciples took notice of Jesus' times of prayer, and they saw the results in the miracles Jesus performed and in the wisdom of his teaching. They were good Jewish boys who had seen many people pray and had prayed often in their own lifetimes, but no one prayed like Jesus. Desiring to follow him in every way, they asked Jesus to teach them how to pray the way he did. The prayer Jesus taught them became one of the most well-known and oft-recited prayers in history. Today we call it the Lord's Prayer, and it starts off, "Our Father in heaven" (Mt 6:9).

Right from the start, Jesus wanted us to focus on the fact that God, the almighty creator of the universe, maker of heaven and earth, is our Father. Whether or not we have ever known the love and protection of an earthly father, we have a Father in heaven who is the perfect ideal on which the concept of fatherhood is based. Jesus reinforced this notion in Luke 11, when he taught the assembled crowd, "Which of you fathers, if your son asks for a fish, will give him a snake instead? Or if he asks for an egg, will give him a scorpion? If you then, though you are evil, know how to give good gifts to your children, how much more will your Father in heaven give the Holy Spirit to those who ask him!" (Lk 11:11-13).

No earthly fathers are perfect, but most of them know enough to give their children things like food that is good to eat instead of snakes and scorpions that can be hurtful and deadly. Jesus was reassuring his listeners that their Father in heaven is absolutely perfect and flawless and gives them only the very best things—in this case, the Holy Spirit, who sustains and comforts us.

FATHER TO THE FATHERLESS

God promises many times in Scripture that he will be a father to the fatherless. In Psalm 10:14, David affirmed that God is specifically on the side of those without fathers: "But you, O God, do see trouble and grief; / you consider it to take it in hand. / The victim commits himself to you; / you are the helper of the fatherless."

Being fatherless is not easy. In Old Testament times, being without a father meant that you were without protection and without provision. When Abraham kicked out Hagar and her son, Ishmael, at the insistence of his wife Sarah, Hagar went as far as she could. Then, out of water and out of hope, she left Ishmael in a shady spot and found another quiet place where she could die without having to watch her son die before her eyes. God miraculously intervened, sending an angel to encourage Hagar and show her a nearby well where she could refresh herself and her son after receiving the Lord's blessing and promise of future prosperity. When the angel arrived, he told Hagar that God had heard Ishmael crying as he lay in the shady place his mother had left him (Gen 21:8-20).

God may not send an angel into our lives to point us toward the nearest water fountain, but he is always ready to answer the cries of his children. Maybe we do not have a father around to help us fix a screen door, change a tire or balance a checkbook. Maybe we have no mother to mend our heart, soothe our troubles or ease our worries. But we can call on our heavenly Father. He is never too busy, never too distracted to give his full attention to one of his children calling his name.

It isn't just in the spiritual things in life that God provides for us. When we pray about the practical issues in our lives—like the broken screen door, the pile of unpaid bills and that crazy sound the car makes—we will be amazed at how God answers! In Matthew 6, Jesus told his disciples not to worry about their clothes or food, not because God is only interested in our spiritual state but because God knows we need physical things, and he will provide for us when we trust him (Mt 6:25-34).

George Müller lived in England in the nineteenth century. Müller came from a good family with connections and wealth, but he wasted everything he was given and stole even more. In his teens he spent time in prison for his misdeeds, but around the age of twenty, Müller met some Christian believers whose shining example set him on a path toward faith in Christ. Eventually Müller dedicated himself to running orphanages, but he has become most famous for his faith-filled prayers.

Müller was convinced that God heard his prayers and that God cared enough to provide for his every need. Instead of holding fundraising campaigns or going on speaking tours to procure funds to feed and clothe and house the thousands of orphans who lived under his care, Müller prayed.

On one well-known occasion, Müller and the children had no food for their breakfast, but Müller prayed in faith, thanking God for the meal they were about to have. Just then, a local baker knocked on the door and reported that he had felt led by God to get up early that morning and bake bread for Müller's family and the orphan children. Müller's extraordinary faith meant that he never told his needs to anyone—except God. He trusted that God would provide everything that was needed, and if God did not provide it, it was not truly needed.

A GUIDING HAND

I have always liked the idea of having someone give me advice. Like many children of divorce, I developed a healthy dose of independence.

But underneath my confident exterior was a desire for someone to put their arm around my shoulders and point out the way.

Perhaps it is part of growing up fast and not wanting to cause trouble when there was already plenty to go around, but many of us seem to be better at doling out advice than seeking it for ourselves. We are the capable ones, the steady rocks in turbulent times. Others come to us in their moments of distress, but we have learned to paste on a tight smile and keep walking when distress comes to our own doorsteps. We learned early that we were on our own. Who do you turn to when you hear your mother cry herself to sleep every night? And why would you ask for one more thing when your father is already trying to cope with a job, a broken heart and a household to run?

When we first meet David in the Bible, he too is very much on his own. The prophet Samuel had been sent by God to anoint a new king of Israel to succeed Saul, after Saul's disobedience cost him the right to have one of his sons follow in his footsteps as king (1 Sam 13:1-14). God told Samuel to go visit Jesse and anoint one of his sons as the next king of the land. When Samuel arrived, Jesse brought out his sons one by one, but Samuel systematically dismissed each one. None of them were God's chosen. Samuel asked Jesse, "Are these all the sons you have?" Either Samuel had heard God wrong or there must be more sons. "'There is still the youngest,' Jesse answered, 'but he is tending the sheep'" (1 Sam 16:11).

In other words Jesse was saying, "I did not think him significant enough for your notice. Surely you cannot mean to choose the youngest son, the one who cares for the family flock, when you have all these strong, fine, handsome young men in front of you." But yes, Samuel—or rather, God—meant to do just that. This one who was the least was the one God had chosen to be king.

David's time in the fields and on the hillsides with the sheep prepared him for his later life. With his shepherd's slingshot, he slew the menacing giant Goliath. Later he spent long stretches of time living in caves and out in the open, on the run from Saul and then from his own son Absalom (1 Sam 18—19; 2 Sam 15). And without David's experience as a shepherd, we would not have the famous Twenty-Third Psalm, which has brought comfort and peace to untold generations.

Yes, David's time with the sheep had a purpose, but it must have been frightening sometimes. Imagine what it was like for David, a young boy out in the wilderness with a bunch of sheep. All those older brothers, but he was so often on his own. There must have been times when he was not sure where to go—literally. A steep, rocky path, a treacherously flooded stream, a dark forest perfect for lions to hide in. Which way was safer for a boy and his sheep? Only God knew.

David learned to rely on God for those decisions. He knew that God would protect him and lead him into safety, even through the most daunting circumstances. Psalm 23:4 says, "Even though I walk / through the valley of the shadow of death, / I will fear no evil." Even in the presence of death itself, in a dark valley full of shadows and danger, David could remain bold and confident because of God's ever-watchful presence. David expressed his confidence in God's leading when he recorded these words that God spoke to him: "I will instruct you and teach you in the way you should go; / I will counsel you and watch over you" (Ps 32:8).

Out on the hillsides, David may have been away from the counsel of his father and older brothers, but he was never alone. Whether it was another boring day in the pasture or a heart-pounding encounter with a lion or bear, God was with David every moment.

My fear of having someone break into my house was magnified in the first place I lived after college. A friend and I rented a small townhouse, and for some reason neither of us ever felt safe there. We never did figure out the reason for our anxiety, but the house gave both of us the creeps. Things came to a head one night when I woke up with an unshakable sense that someone was on the stairway coming up to the second floor, where our bedrooms were. I sat bolt upright in bed and began praying furiously. I was frozen in place, all my careful plans of hiding or running or fighting back paralyzed by fear. After some minutes of intense prayer, I felt a sudden calm, an assurance that everything was fine. I glanced at the clock next to my bed, noting the time, then lay back down and went peacefully to sleep.

The next morning my roommate told me she had had a weird experience the night before. She had woken up, certain someone was on the staircase. She too had looked at the clock. It was the same time that I had awoken with the same feeling. Talk about creepy. If it had been hard to sleep in that townhouse before, it felt nearly impossible after that incident.

Shortly after this, I was reading in the Psalms and came across this verse: "I will lie down and sleep in peace, / for you alone, O LORD, / make me dwell in safety" (Ps 4:8). It was just the assurance I needed. I embroidered the verse on some fabric and hung it above my bed where I could see it every night.

Most commentators believe David wrote Psalm 4 when he was on the run from King Saul. Having been anointed by Samuel to succeed Saul, David became an inevitable and inescapable threat to Saul's dreams of a dynasty. So the hunt was on. Saul and his army chased David and his small band of supporters over hill and dale, all through the mountains and caves and valleys of Israel. Not yet a king, David had no fortress to which he could retreat, no castle where he could bring up the drawbridge and stare Saul down across an alligator-laden moat. Instead, David and his men slept out in the open, sheltered by rocks and caves, taking turns keeping watch during the night, listening for the sound of snapping twigs or looking for telltale signs of a nearby campfire.

How vulnerable they must have felt, especially David, who had already twice escaped being pinned to a wall by Saul's spear.

It was under these circumstances that David penned the words, "I will lie down and sleep in peace, for you alone, O LORD, make me dwell in safety." When I read those words at that time in my life, I decided that if David could trust God to keep him safe from harm under such obviously dangerous conditions, then surely I could trust the same God to keep me safe behind a locked door and tucked snugly in my own warm bed. All the locks and security systems and barking dogs in the world could not keep me safer than the ever-watchful eye of my God, the same God who kept a shepherd-turned-king safe from lions and bears and murderous kings.

JUSTIFIED FEARS

Since I was five years old, I have had a stepfather—someone who carried me to bed when I pretended to fall asleep on the sofa while watching TV, someone who taught me to fish, taught me to drive a manual transmission (while my brothers laughed mercilessly in the back seat), someone who was always ready with a helpful lecture about any topic at hand.

Not everyone is so fortunate. Marquardt writes:

> More than seventy reputable studies document that an astonishing number—anywhere from one-third to one-half—of girls with divorced parents report having been molested or sexually abused as children, often by their mothers' boyfriends or stepfathers. A separate review of forty-two studies found that "the majority of children who were sexually abused . . . appeared to come from single-parent or reconstituted families." Two leading researchers in the field conclude, "Living with a stepparent has turned out to be the most powerful predictor of severe child abuse yet."[7]

Some of the people I interviewed fall into that category. They lived with the constant fear of a raised fist or a nighttime visit, their childhood gone amid the terror of a very real threat. They were not just comforting a mother who missed her husband, they were comforting a mother who was nursing a black eye and wondering if the storm of anger had blown over or if there was more fury yet to be unleashed. They pulled sheets protectively over themselves at night, hoping this would be one night they could sleep alone and unharmed. For these children of divorce, fear was rooted in a very painful reality.

Back in the early 1990s, Amy Grant sang about a girl who was suffering from sexual abuse. The haunting lyrics questioned where God was while she endured shame. There is no easy answer to that question. Where is God when we experience the unspeakable? Amy Grant's song went on to say that God was right there with this girl, even in the middle of her shame and abject terror. We've already learned that God cares for us and that he is strong enough to help us in any situation. So why did he not help these children? Why did he allow them to suffer abuse and unspeakable harm?

We are given a small, enigmatic hint at the answers in the book of Job. In what some believe to be the earliest book of the Bible, we see a drama played out in the heavens. Satan bargains with God for the right to torment an innocent man. God stops short of letting Satan kill Job, but he leaves everything else pretty much up for grabs. Satan wipes out Job's accumulated wealth in one stroke, then kills all of his children at once, then inflicts him with painful boils from head to toe. In the process, Job's reputation is ruined since his friends and neighbors can think of no reason God would allow all of these horrible things to happen in Job's life unless he had committed some awful, hidden sin that he was refusing to confess. Job's wife—that paragon of spousal support—tells Job to curse God and die!

Where was Job's hope? Certainly not in the present. In the midst of his agony, he looked beyond the immediate and foresaw the Messiah. He said, "Even now my witness is in heaven; / my advocate is on high. / My intercessor is my friend / as my eyes pour out tears to God; / on behalf of a man he pleads with God / as a man pleads for his friend" (Job 16:19-21). He may not have known why all of this was happening, but Job knew that he had an intercessor, an advocate, who was pleading his case before God.

Eventually God answers Job, and at first glance it is one of the most unsatisfying answers imaginable. We would like God to show up and make sense of it all, to give a perfectly logical explanation for the whole mess—at the very least, to tell Job what wonderful spiritual truths God has been teaching Job through this experience. But that is not what God does.

Instead, God shows up and hands Job his celestial resume. His reasoning is that of a parent who says, "Because I said so." God essentially tells Job, "When you are big enough and wise enough to create a magnificent universe and keep it rolling along perfectly for a couple of millennia, then you can begin to question me. Until then, let's remember who is the Creator and who is the created."

It is not the answer we are looking for, but ultimately it is the only answer we get from a God who is beyond our understanding. And it is the only answer that offers real comfort. How can it be comforting? Because we know that, indeed, our God made everything that exists; he is sovereign over all of creation, including us, and not one tiny thing that happens escapes his notice or thwarts his plans. The horrible things that sometimes happen in the secrecy of our families, in homes where we should have been safe, have not been secret from God, nor will they remain secret. Paul says that God will one day judge us and "bring to light what is hidden in darkness" (1 Cor 4:5).

Jesus told his followers that they should trust God's providential care, even when times got tough, even when their lives were threatened. He said, "Do not be afraid of those who kill the body but cannot kill the soul. Rather, be afraid of the One who can destroy both soul and body in hell. Are not two sparrows sold for a penny? Yet not one of them will fall to the ground apart from the will of your Father" (Mt 10:28-29).

The knowledge that God has it all under control brings peace. I am not responsible for ordering my world; at the same time, those around me have no ability to do anything to me that God is not fully aware of and that he has not allowed and ordained.

Jesus knew this. After being flogged by Roman soldiers until he was so bloodied and mangled that he was barely recognizable, he stood calmly before Pontius Pilate. Convinced Jesus was innocent, and afraid that he might actually be a god, Pilate tried to get Jesus to give him some defense, some reason not to condemn him. In desperation, Pilate asked Jesus, "Don't you realize I have power either to free you or to crucify you?" (Jn 19:10).

Undaunted, Jesus replied, "You would have no power over me if it were not given to you from above" (Jn 19:11). Every cruelty inflicted on Christ at the hands of human beings was part of God's plan for our redemption and healing. Because Jesus was absolutely certain of God's love and of his sovereign purpose, he could confidently face the horror and agony of that awful day.

Jesus' confidence in God gave him peace and security during what would otherwise have been a terrifying experience. We can live in that same calm assurance. As Paul writes in Philippians 4:7, "The peace of God, which transcends all understanding, will guard your hearts and your minds in Christ Jesus."

This peace is not one that depends on our outward circumstances. It is a peace we have in spite of our outward circumstances. Lynn feels that peace in her life now. Although she never experienced abuse or lived in fear, she found herself consumed by anger and bitterness many years after her parents' divorce. It began when Lynn became a mother herself and tried to understand how her own mother could have abandoned their family. The rage she felt toward her mother overshadowed her joy in being a mother and robbed Lynn of her peace.

It wasn't until Lynn realized that God had made peace with her through his offer of salvation through the death of Jesus that she began to release her anger. Lynn had been a Christian for many years, but she had never connected the grace God had given her spiritually with the grace she needed to deal with her parents' divorce. Slowly Lynn came to realize that God was in control of her situation. As she began to focus more and more on God's love for her, she focused less and less on the anger she felt toward her mother. She says, "For me that is where the healing is taking and has taken place; the more I realize my identity in Christ, as a child of God, the less I view myself as a child of divorce."

Lynn's circumstances did not radically change, but God gave her his peace in the midst of her circumstances. That is the way his peace often works—defying logic, surrounding us with protection when we ought to feel the most stressed. He has promised us children of divorce this peace.

All Things Made New

While I was growing up, I adored my father. Perhaps it was easy to do so since I only saw him for a few weeks each year. But there really was a lot to adore. My father is handsome and charming and witty. He likes to have goofy fun, he has an artistic flair and long ago he acquired an urban sophistication. When I was little, he would take pictures of me from all different angles like I was a model posing for *Vogue*, then hand over the camera and ham it up while I snapped a few shots of him. He bought me my first tape recorder and encouraged me to record my thoughts and conduct interviews. He was my first interview subject, and I still giggle when I listen to the tape and hear his purposefully silly answers to my very serious questions.

By the time I was a teenager, I knew Dad was not perfect. For one thing, he was a procrastinator and was often late. I remember once running through LAX desperately trying to get to the gate before boarding closed, while Dad waited for my bags to go through security and then ran after me. (I made it, but just barely.) And he was not the most practical guy. One fun day at the beach with him resulted in the two of us lounging in agony in front of fans, our skin the color of just-boiled lobsters because Dad did not bring sunblock and I was too young to think of it myself.

Still, if ever a girl thought her father walked on clouds, it was me. And then he disappeared in the clouds, and I didn't see him for eight long years. When I did finally see him again, he tried to get me to call him Bill instead of Dad. I remember the first few times I saw him after those eight years, when the walls that had been erected were slowly being dismantled. There were some awkward moments, some tentative conversations. Something in our relationship was broken, shattered, and while we were picking up the pieces and slowly applying glue, there were still a lot of jagged edges and missing parts.

As we began rebuilding our father-daughter relationship, I found myself always wanting more. Every interaction I had with Dad left me disappointed. It was like getting a small sip of water when what I really wanted was to gulp down a full bottle to slake my thirst. Then I read Dr. Kevin Leman's book *Making Sense of the Men in Your Life,* and I realized that I was carrying around an expectation of my dad that he was not meeting. I wanted him to be Father of the Year, to suddenly turn into Pa Ingalls or Ward Cleaver. The pastor of a church I once attended was fond of saying, "The difference between reality and expectation is disappointment." He was right. Leman put it this way: "You know that latent sense that you've always been missing something but you were never sure exactly what it was? Well, this is it. This is the father you've always wanted, pitted against the father you've always had."[1]

Reading those words was a breakthrough for me. I realized that my dad had never been the superstar I had made him out to be. He was not the creature from the black lagoon, but neither was he Ward Cleaver. I needed to stop holding my dad responsible for not being the father I wanted him to be and start appreciating and enjoying the father he is. My dad is probably never going to engage me in deep conversations about my life, give me fatherly advice about men and ask how my car is running. But he is still a charming and witty man who makes me laugh and encourages my talents.

There is another side to this equation too: I have a stepfather. We do not share the same DNA, but we have history, the memories of our shared family experiences, and I know that he is always more than happy to have those big conversations, to dispense the fatherly advice and to make sure my car is running well. His presence in my life is a comfort and a blessing to me.

Some of the people I talked to as I was writing this book had stepfathers who later disappeared just as their fathers had. Some had mothers who left and never returned.

After Derrick's parents divorced, his mother remarried, but Derrick did not enjoy a close relationship with either his dad or his stepfather. As he began to approach marriage in his early thirties, Derrick struggled with fear. He felt that he had never had a good model for what a husband should be. But Derrick recognized his fear and decided to do something about it. He began spending time with a Christian man whose family he admired. When Derrick had fears about marriage or questions about how one went about being a good husband or a good father, he had long talks with his mentor. But mostly he spent time observing.

Derrick did purposefully what author Donald Miller did by accident. Miller did not adopt his mentor, John MacMurray. It was the other way around. MacMurray and his wife invited Miller to live in the apartment over their garage. Although he was not looking for an example of godly manhood, Miller got a front-row seat. Reflecting back on the experience, Miller wrote, "For the first time in my life, I saw what a father does, what a father teaches a kid, what a husband does around the house, the way a man interacts with the world around him, the way a man—just as does a woman—holds a family together."[2]

Just because we have grown up in homes the world refers to as broken does not mean that we have to remain broken for the rest of our lives. Yes, there have been a lot of broken, shattered things in our lives, and sometimes sharp fragments are still lying around, waiting to prick us in unsuspecting moments. But we do not have to live in a constant and lifelong state of disarray and destruction. An atomic bomb was dropped on our family, but with time, new green shoots of life can spring up from the charred wreckage.

THE BLIGHT OF THE LOCUSTS

The first chapter of the book written by the Old Testament prophet Joel tells a tale of utter desolation. "What the locust swarm has left / the great locusts have eaten; / what the great locusts have left / the young locusts have eaten; / what the young locusts have left / other locusts have eaten" (Joel 1:4).

This was no ordinary event. There were locusts on top of locusts on top of locusts. This plague of insects made the Egyptian plague of Moses' day look like one solitary bug.

On the Banks of Plum Creek by Laura Ingalls Wilder tells the true story of swarms of locusts that obliterated the sun and destroyed two years of wheat in nineteenth-century Minnesota. Over a period of five years, locusts destroyed more than thirteen million bushels of wheat and eleven million bushels of corn and oats.[3] Wilder wrote of her own experience: "Huge brown grasshoppers were hitting the ground all around her, hitting her head and her face and her arms. They came thudding down like hail. The cloud was hailing grasshoppers. The cloud *was* grasshoppers. Their bodies hid the sun and made darkness. Their thin, large wings gleamed and glittered. The rasping whirring of their wings filled the whole air and they hit the ground and the house with the noise of a hailstorm."[4] Before it was over, Wilder wrote, the wheat and oats—their cash crops—were destroyed that year, their vegetable garden was gone and there was no grass for the milk cows to eat.

Westminster Theological Seminary professor Raymond Dillard writes of the passage in Joel that even today a large swarm of locusts can devastate a region. Once the crops are destroyed, food becomes scarce, lowering the immune systems of the starving people and making them more vulnerable to disease. The scarcity of food prevents the affected area from trading its surpluses, driving up prices and weakening the economy. Once the locusts die, their rotting carcasses breed typhus and other communicable diseases. Dillard goes on to say that swarms "have even been observed twelve hundred miles at sea. The swarms can reach great sizes: a swarm across the Red Sea in 1889 was estimated to cover two thousand square miles. A swarm is estimated to contain up to 120 million insects per mile."[5] Imagine a swarm of locusts roughly the size of Delaware's land mass! With so many ravenous insects, not a single piece of vegetation would be left. In fact, as Hampton Keathley points out, the locusts Joel talks about would have destroyed even the grain that the Israelites used in their grain offerings to the Lord, meaning "their sacrifices had to stop and their relationship with God was severed."[6] In other words, this proclamation by the prophet Joel tells us everything that mattered had been destroyed.

The loss of our families can make us feel this way—forsaken and utterly destroyed. We can feel like that wheat field next to the Little House on the Prairie, stripped bare and good for nothing. The family we knew is gone, blown apart, obliterated. Maybe more than just our family was gone. For many of us, divorce meant leaving the house we grew up in, leaving our neighborhood, our friends, our school. For some of us, divorce even meant losing our church, either because we felt ashamed that our family did not fit the image we thought everyone expected of us or because we felt and even heard condemnation from those who should have been most concerned for our souls. To use Joel's metaphor, locusts ate our family, but then other locusts came and ate our friendships and childhood home, and still more locusts ate our church.

But there is more to the book of Joel. We need to keep reading. Joel did not write just one chapter. There was destruction and famine and hopelessness for a time, but God did not leave his people in such a state.

In chapter 2, God offered this promise:

> I will repay you for the years the locusts have eaten—
>> the great locust and the young locust,
>> the other locusts and the locust swarm—
> my great army that I sent among you.
> You will have plenty to eat, until you are full,
>> and you will praise the name of the LORD your God,
>> who has worked wonders for you;
> never again will my people be shamed. (Joel 2:25-26)

What a great promise! God does not promise that we will eke out a living from the dusty earth left behind by the locusts. He says we will have an abundance, that we will eat until we are full. It is like the children's Sunday school song that says "he feeds me at his banqueting table." The tables are overflowing with good things to eat, more than we can possibly need, and God invites us to sit down and eat until we cannot eat another bite. God is not stingy with his blessing. He promises to fully restore the lost years and bring us to a place where we will be completely satisfied. This is a lifeline, a hope we can hold on to when things look bleak.

I cannot tell you what that restoration will look like in your life, nor can I tell you when it will happen. Some of us will see broken relationships with our parents and siblings mended and new ones forged that are stronger and deeper. Others of us will build our own great marriages and loving families that will bring us tremendous joy. And some of us may have to wait for heaven, where all wrongs will be righted, all wounds healed, all tears wiped away.

One man I talked to described the announcement of his parents' divorce as his family's own personal 9/11. "We were sitting in the house, secure and safe, watching television, not suspecting a thing; and then suddenly, wham! You turn away from the television for a minute and think, 'I couldn't have just seen that; it couldn't have been real.' But then you turn back to look and see it all replayed, over and over again." He is still waiting for the restoration to begin in his life, to see God bring him to a place of feasting after the blight of locusts. What he has seen, however, is that God has used his ministry to urban youth to teach him about the power of persistent, unconditional love to break down walls of insincerity and falsehood. He is trying to apply this principle to his relationship with his father and hopes that he will one day see his father come clean with him about the real story behind his abandonment of their family.

Like this man, and like most of the people I interviewed for this book, I too am still in the process of healing, of watching the young green shoots poke through the barren soil. I do not have a perfect relationship with my dad, but we talk from time to time, and each time it is less awkward and less stressful. It has not been easy and it has not been quick, but the locusts are not having the last word!

When we are still in the locust-stripped field, we need to re-member that God knows where we are. Think about all the great people in the Bible who encountered God or his emissaries: Abraham, who entertained angels in his tent home (Gen 18); Jacob, who saw the ladder to heaven with angels ascending and descend-ing (Gen 28:10-22); Moses, who saw God in a burning bush (Ex 3); Daniel, whose prayer was answered by a visit from the angel Gabriel (Dan 9); the virgin Mary, who received a special message of her own from Gabriel (Lk 1:26-38). In not one of these passages do we read that the angel got lost or had to ask around for directions.

God did not burn up ten bushes on random mountains hoping that Moses would stumble across his path. None of the angels says, "Oh, there you are! I've been looking everywhere for you!" Even Gabriel, who had to stop and fight a battle on his way to deliver his message to Daniel, knew exactly where to find him. God knows exactly where we are. He knows it geographically, he knows it spiritually, he knows it emotionally. Your bare, locust-eaten field of a heart is no surprise to him, nor has it escaped his notice.

There is an old spiritual that says, "Nobody knows the trouble I've seen." Part of us is actually glad that nobody knows our deepest trouble. We do not like the vulnerability of letting others see the anguish of our souls laid bare. In many Christian circles, it can be very tempting to paste on a smile and pretend that nothing in the world is troubling us. This is shallow Christianity, and it masks the truth. If we could see into the lives of those other nicely dressed and pressed members of our churches, we would see many wounds and scars as deep as our own. Life does that to us, but sorrow is not all bad. I am convinced that without deep sorrow, deep joy and deep peace are not possible.

TESTING THE LINE

I joined a women's outdoor club a few years ago. I loved the opportunity to learn new skills in classes designed for women. My favorite activity was sea kayaking. We learned to finesse our strokes, not power through them like men might, and we learned that a woman's lower center of gravity helps anchor the kayak better than a man's bulky upper-body strength. I even participated in a one-day rock-climbing class, which was a real stretch for me because I have a well-rooted fear of heights.

I had already taken enough classes with this group to know that the instructors were top-notch. Still, scaling a forty-foot rock wall left me with sweaty palms and trembling legs. The instructors were prepared. The first thing they had each of us do was gear up, strap ourselves into our safety harnesses and climb up about ten feet. Then we were instructed to let go. The idea was for each of us to test the harness and belay system, and the person holding our belay rope on the ground, and also to teach us what to do in the event of a fall. We learned that our hands and feet should be outstretched but not stiff—like a Spider-Man pose—to keep us from slamming face first into the side of the cliff. Our job was to fall, in all its terror, and learn that it was okay, we would survive, the rope would hold, the person at the bottom would not let us go crashing to the ground.

Once we completed our practice fall, we felt freedom—freedom to reach for the ledge that was no wider than our fingertips or to stretch for the toehold that, if we could just reach it, would get us where we wanted to go next. We felt freedom because we knew that if we lost our grip, if our fingers and toes could not keep us upright, we would fall, but only a few short feet. Then we could start right back up the wall. Experiencing that fear and utter loss of control, and discovering that everything would be fine after all, was the only way to climb with absolute confidence.

That is the confidence we have with God. There may be times when we lose our grip and go spinning wildly, but we are not like those crazy people who free-climb without equipment. We are tethered securely, strapped into a belay system with God on the other end, letting out slack and pulling it in, standing with his feet planted and his strong arms taut when we take a tumble. Just as I did when I was ten feet up the cliff on my first test climb, we can let go and test the ropes. God will not let us fall.

Horatio Spafford wrote the words to the beloved hymn "It Is Well with My Soul." What great words of confidence and strength: "When peace like a river attendeth my way." The next line, though, begins to tell us the real story: "When sorrows like sea billows roll."

Spafford and his wife were mourning the death of their only son when the Chicago fire of 1871 also devastated them financially. Spafford was a wealthy man, but his wealth was nearly all in real estate, and he literally watched it go up in smoke. The family was reeling from these two tragedies, so he decided they needed a vacation. With business still to attend to, Spafford put his wife and four daughters onto an ocean liner to Europe, planning to join them soon after. But during their ocean passage, tragedy struck yet again. The ship carrying Spafford's family collided with another ship. He received an ominous telegram from his wife: "Saved alone." All four of his daughters had died, along with more than two hundred others.

Spafford boarded a ship for England, where his wife awaited him. Like Job, Spafford suffered the additional loss of his reputation, as friends and strangers wondered what he had done to offend God and bring so much loss on himself. But when the ship's captain summoned Spafford and told him they were now at the spot where the collision was believed to have taken place, Spafford was filled not with despair but with hope. "It is well, it is well with my soul," he wrote. His daughter Bertha, born five years after these sad events, later wrote, "That he could write such words at such a time was made possible by the fierceness of his struggle and the completeness of the victory."[7]

If ever anyone tested the strength of the ropes, it was Spafford. Reeling, spinning, falling helplessly, he found that he was safely strapped in after all, held securely by God. It was a fierce struggle, but the victory was complete.

Ecclesiastes reminds us that "there is a time for everything, / and a season for every activity under heaven: / . . . a time to weep and a time to laugh" (Eccles 3:1, 4). As Spafford found, joy and peace often follow trouble and sorrow.

In the first chapter of this book, we considered the joy that comes from knowing that God sees our deepest sorrows. David reminds us in Psalm 31:7, "I will be glad and rejoice in your love, / for you saw my affliction / and knew the anguish of my soul." David goes on to talk about God's merciful provision, his "wonderful love," his refuge and great goodness. He ends the psalm by saying, "Be strong and take heart, / all you who hope in the LORD" (v. 24). God's knowledge of our sorrow is cause for rejoicing because he is a just God and will restore the years the locusts have eaten.

DRY BONES LIVE AGAIN

There is no sorrow, no desolation beyond the reach of God's restoring power. The Lord demonstrated this forcefully through one of his more eccentric prophets. The prophet Ezekiel was given what can only be described as a lot of really weird object lessons and visions.

The book of Ezekiel begins with a vision Ezekiel was given of a strange wheel within a wheel. A gyroscope of sorts, it was made up of a ball of fire enveloping four humanlike creatures, each of which had four faces—human, lion, ox and eagle—and four wings (Ezek 1:15-28). And then it got weirder.

Ezekiel was told to eat a book (Ezek 3:1-2). Seriously. Then God told him to build a model of Jerusalem under siege, using a drawing, a brick and a skillet (Ezek 4:1-3). He baked bread over a fire of smoldering dung (Ezek 4:9-15). He cut his beard and hair with a sword, burned one third of it, chopped up one third to sprinkle around the city and threw one third to the wind (Ezek 5:1-4). And after all this, God told Ezekiel that he would be part of a terrible object lesson, that a very costly sacrifice would be demanded of him in God's service: God caused Ezekiel's wife, the delight of his life, to die (Ezek 24:15-18).

God had Ezekiel working overtime to try to get his message across to the people of Israel. And while Ezekiel definitely got the attention of the people around him, he also felt lonely and misunderstood, for reasons we can well imagine. But God also gave Ezekiel some incredible visions. The last portion of Ezekiel is a detailed description of his visit in vision form to the temple of God in what seems to be the New Jerusalem (Ezek 40—48). He saw the glory of God filling the temple and pouring out through the gates. What an encouragement that must have been for Ezekiel, to see this God of hard lessons and sometimes odd demands in all his glory, and how humbling and awe-inspiring for this prophet who gave so much of himself to preach God's message.

Most of these stories from Ezekiel are left out of children's Sunday school curricula. But there is one portion of Ezekiel that many of us are familiar with—the dry bones.

God took Ezekiel to a vast open area covered with human bones. These were not fresh corpses from yesterday's bloody battle. These were parched bones on the desert floor, the kind of skeletons that pop out at Indiana Jones on his dangerous ventures to let him know that a hundred years earlier someone else tried, unsuccessfully, to steal this treasure. John Gill's commentary on this passage of Ezekiel says, "And, lo, they were very dry, through length of time they had lain there, exposed to wind and weather; the flesh being wholly consumed from off of them, and the marrow within quite dried up; so that there was no probability or hope, humanly speaking, of their being quickened."[8] While his language is antiquated, I like his description of the bones: dry, weather-beaten, without a shred of flesh, without marrow, beyond hope of reviving.

Standing before this field of dried, bleached bones, God had a simple question for the prophet: "Son of man, can these bones live?" (Ezek 37:3). A field stripped bare by locusts is one thing, but a valley full of dry bones? Can we really expect them to live again?

The confidence of the prophet Ezekiel is both humorous and encouraging. In response to God's question, Ezekiel—not seeing how it was possible, but trusting God to be able to do anything—simply said, "O Sovereign LORD, you alone know!" It is as if Ezekiel were saying, "I'm doubtful, but I've seen you do weirder things, God! And this sounds like a trick question."

God had Ezekiel prophesy that the bones would live, that they would again have muscle and flesh on them, that they would be alive in every sense of the word. "As I prophesied, there was a sound and, oh, rustling! The bones moved and came together, bone to bone. I kept watching. Sinews formed, then muscles on the bones, then skin stretched over them. But they had no breath in them" (Ezek 37:7-8 *The Message*). God was not finished. He told Ezekiel to prophesy again, to summon breath for the bones that now had flesh but no life. "So I prophesied, just as he commanded me. The breath entered them and they came alive! They stood up on their feet, a huge army" (Ezek 37:10 *The Message*).

God gave Ezekiel this message to Israel at a time when they were without hope. He wanted them to know that he would rescue them from their lifeless situation and breathe into them his own life. And he kept the promise. He rescued his Old Testament people from captivity, and he gave to Israel and to us his own life on the cross and his own Spirit at Pentecost.

God's message to Ezekiel and to Israel was that even a valley full of dry bones was not beyond hope. Most of us, including me, have felt like a pile of dry bones at one time or another in our lives. Parched, left in the desert, we can feel devoid of life and depleted of any hope for restoration.

No matter how bone-dry we feel in our spirit, no matter how hopeless our situation looks, God has to do no more than speak a few words for life to return. We can spring to our feet and be ready for action, like the army that arose from that arid plain of carcasses.

This is not something we have to do on our own. In fact, we cannot do it on our own. Only God can put new life into a heart that has lost its life. God does this work in us when we seek him. He carries us through the tough times to a place of abundance.

Another prophet of God says, "So do not fear, for I am with you; / do not be dismayed, for I am your God. / I will strengthen you and help you; / I will uphold you with my righteous right hand" (Is 41:10). God's right hand is the hand of strength and honor. With it, he will hold us safe and secure, leading us toward the restoration of our hearts, our families, our lives.

The psalmist was confident of God's power to restore: "Though you have made me see troubles, many and bitter, / you will restore my life again; / from the depths of the earth you will again bring me up. / You will increase my honor and comfort me once again" (Ps 71:20-21). These are words of real comfort. The psalmist did not latch onto a false expectation that God would always make his life rosy or keep all sorrow from him. The troubles he saw were "many and bitter." But he knew that they would not last, that God would bring him back to a place of plenty and praise. This language is resurrection language. He paints a picture of life being restored, of a person being raised up, like the dry bones in Ezekiel's vision. Charles Spurgeon wrote, "However low the Lord may permit us to sink, he will fix a limit to the descent, and in due time will bring us up again. Even when we are laid low in the tomb, the mercy is that we can go no lower, but shall retrace our steps and mount to better lands; and all this, because the Lord is ever mighty to save. A little God would fail us, but not Jehovah the Omnipotent."[9]

I love that last sentence! We follow after so many gods, trying to find satisfaction, wholeness, fulfillment. We subject ourselves to the petty demands of petty idols and spin our wheels trying to satisfy a little god who is as needy as we are. Sometimes our god is worry: "What if my parents' divorce has doomed me to a life of failed relationships?" Sometimes we worship at the temple of the god of resentment or leave offerings at the shrine of the god of fear and despair.

The Lord—Jehovah the Omnipotent—is not like those gods. As Exodus 15:11 says, "Who among the gods is like you, O LORD?" The answer is, "There is none like you!" (Ps 86:8). This great, magnificent, powerful God can redeem us from a life of servitude to our false gods, and he restores us to life.

NEW CLOTHES, SINGING AND LAUGHING

Some of us move beyond pain only to go to a place of numbness. Like overmedicated patients on strong painkillers, we no longer cry out from sharp pangs and stabs of hurt, but the medicine that keeps us pain-free also keeps us from feeling much of anything else. Our pain-free state is a hard compromise. We may not be miserable anymore, but neither are we truly happy. It's a little like the Buddhist answer to pain—just stop wanting anything. But to stop wanting anything, we have to be willing to give up the good things, like joy and happiness and redemption.

God has a different plan for our recovery. He does not ask us to stop craving but rather to crave something different—him. And he promises that in finding him, we will find all those other things we desire. As Jesus said, "Seek first his kingdom and his righteousness, and all these things will be given to you as well" (Mt 6:33).

David, the king of Israel, put it this way, "You turned my wailing into dancing; / you removed my sackcloth and clothed me with joy, / that my heart may sing to you and not be silent. / O LORD my God, I will give you thanks forever" (Ps 30:11-12). David had a right to speak those words. The songs he wrote, pouring out his heart to God, speak movingly of his despair and anguish as life piled on disappointment and heartache. His sin with Bathsheba caused their infant son to die (2 Sam 12:13-19). His son Amnon raped David's daughter Tamar (2 Sam 13:1-22). To avenge his sister, David's son Absalom murdered Amnon (2 Sam 13:23-33), only to be killed later by David's supporters after leading a rebellion against his father (2 Sam 18:1-18). Talk about a dysfunctional family! David had good cause to spend some time wailing and wearing sackcloth. But this man who experienced some truly horrific family dynamics could sing praise to God and affirm that God had redeemed and transformed his times of sorrow, giving him instead times of joy and elation.

Even Job's friends, little consolation that they were, reminded him of God's tender care and restorative power: "He will yet fill your mouth with laughter / and your lips with shouts of joy" (Job 8:21). These are sweet and tender words. God does not go halfway. He does not just ease our pain—he replaces it with joy, singing, laughing and shouting. He will work this transformation in our hearts if we will let him.

How do we get to a place of restoration? It starts with giving God our pain—telling him about it, acknowledging it and releasing it into his care, trusting him to bring goodness and wholeness out of it. Some of us have not done that. We have buried our pain or held onto it, nursing it and pulling it out to look at in moments of anger or self-pity. We need to let go of it, but the answer is not to toss it to the wind. The answer is to give it to God, because he is trustworthy. He will not lose it or toss it aside or handle it carelessly. God is like an avant-garde artist who takes the trash of our brokenness and turns it into a sculpture that inspires and delights. We can let go of it once for all and trust him to do a good work with it.

Although it may be difficult to imagine right now, God promises that our sadness will not last forever. We can look forward with eager expectation to the day we will find laughter and joy again. It will come, and it will be better than anything we thought possible!

Spend some time right now thinking deeply about how you will be restored. Get a piece of paper and write about how you will feel when the sadness has passed and joy has returned, or imagine what it will be like to dance with a heart that is not burdened down with sorrow. Remember, "Weeping may remain for a night, / but rejoicing comes in the morning" (Ps 30:5).

More Than a Statistic

A few years ago I helped teach a Sunday school class for children whose parents were divorced or divorcing. Once the curriculum was put together and we were ready to begin, we needed to make a sign for our classroom so the children and their parents would know where we were meeting. The trouble was, we could not agree on a name for the class. Some wanted a generic name like "Rainbow Kids," something that would convey hope and not advertise the real nature of the class and make the children feel singled out. Others argued for the simple and straightforward "Children of Divorce Class." We still had not decided on a name when the day of the first class rolled around, so we decided to ask the children what they thought. Their unanimous vote was for "Children of Divorce." They did not want to hide behind an ambiguous name.

I thought the class's decision, and the angst it created in some of the adults, was telling. Those of us in Generations X and Y who are children of divorce and churchgoers typically found little conversation about our family structure in religious settings. For the most part we were ignored. Occasionally we were ostracized. There was a stigma attached to being a child of divorced parents, and we learned to keep it under wraps. (The young kids in my Sunday school class, however, had either not yet caught on to the stigma or were experiencing a different generational reality.)

Part of this stigma comes from the statistics that are floating around. Depending on what you read, we children of divorce are more likely than our peers to run away from home, drop out of school, abuse drugs and alcohol, commit suicide, have children out of wedlock, never marry, get divorced, be on welfare and live shorter lives. One article I saw even concluded that the stress of divorce could stunt the growth of children, (though let me assure you, I come by my diminutive height quite naturally).[1]

While statistics can be informative and helpful, they also have a down side. The danger is that we can feel defined, even doomed, by those statistics. Are we destined to be forever relationship-challenged, at-risk, even short? Okay, so I may not be able to change that last one except with a good pair of stilettos. Is there hope for us, though? And if there is, where do we find it? How can we grab hold of it and make it our reality?

Hope is a powerful force. It sustains us when times are tough, helping us keep a smile on our face and a spring in our step when circumstances are not perfect. On the flip side, lack of hope is every bit as powerful. The Proverbs say, "Hope deferred makes the heart sick" (Prov 13:12). Feeling hopeless sucks the wind out of our sails.

I felt the wind leave my sails when I first read Judith Wallerstein's *The Unexpected Legacy of Divorce*. It was the first book I read on children of divorce, so it was the first time I saw many of the statistics and began to understand some of the ways we approach life differently than people from intact homes. One story in particular, which I shared in chapter four, riveted my attention. Wallerstein contrasts two women, Lisa and Bettina. Lisa's parents were divorced. She drifted from relationship to relationship, resolute in her decision not to marry and risk betrayal. But Wallerstein saw beyond the protective façade Lisa erected, commenting, "Lisa's decision was coming not so much from disinterest in an intimate relationship as from her fear that trust and love were beyond her reach."[2]

Lisa had been the maid of honor at her friend Bettina's wedding. Bettina grew up with parents who had stayed married, and Wallerstein interviewed her at Lisa's suggestion. Bettina's expectations of finding love were very different from her friend's. She told Wallerstein, "I never doubted that I would find a good man to love me and to love in return."[3] What most separated these two young women was hope. Bettina had hope that buoyed her and gave her confidence, while Lisa's fragile hope provided a tenuous lifeline to romance.

Matt Daniels, one of the early drafters of traditional marriage legislation, came from a broken home, a background that drove his passion for emphasizing the importance of traditional families. Citing his lack of a role model for what it meant to be a husband and father, Daniels called his marriage in 1995 "an act of faith."[4]

Mark was in high school when his parents divorced. When they told their children they were getting a divorce, Mark thought they were joking. When he realized they were serious, he felt betrayed. His parents were churchgoers who had instilled two rules into their kids: don't have sex before marriage, and don't divorce. Not only did his parents divorce, but Mark suspects that his father may have been having an affair with the woman he later married.

Seeing his parents break the rules they had always preached to their children disillusioned Mark. He says he simply lost hope. Mark became a party animal, determined to drown the hopeless feelings that engulfed him. The police had to break up several parties he had in high school, and he consciously decided to spend his college years having as much fun as possible. Looking back, he realizes that God spared his life during some particularly harrowing drunken experiences he had at that time.

Two years after college graduation, Mark gave his life unreservedly to Christ. He gave up his partying lifestyle, and today he approaches life and relationships with confidence and hope. Like some of the other children of divorce I spoke with, Mark realizes that marriage takes work, that it requires communication and that God must be at the center of it. Mark will soon have the chance to put that knowledge into practical use, as he recently became engaged to be married.

Mark was the most hopeful child of divorce that I interviewed. I talked with people who were single and people who were married, people whose parents had divorced many years ago and people for whom the sting of a recently broken family was still sharp. Most could identify specific areas of their lives in which they still struggled, stemming from either the breakup of their parents' marriage or a difficult relationship with one or both parents.

True to the research, many of us did face new challenges as we entered adulthood and began forming our own romantic attachments. For some, the disappointments piled on until hope was buried so deeply that it seemed gone forever. Others simply learned to live day by day, to take life as it comes and not look too closely into the future. This may help us avoid the disappointment of the future not living up to our expectations, but in the process we also avoid the joy of hope.

So how do we live in hope, not defined by statistics that say we have a slim chance of succeeding at marriage and at life? I think we know that Lisa, Judith Wallerstein's subject, had the wrong answer. By avoiding marriage, Lisa thought she could control her world and avoid betrayal and disappointment. In reality, she only managed to experience betrayal and disappointment in dating relationships.

The fact is, we cannot perfectly control our worlds. Bad things do happen to good people, and sometimes the most ordered lives can come crashing down with little warning. People betray us, economies rise and fall, health flourishes and wanes. The solution lies not in carefully controlling our lives but in trusting God. Only he can control our futures. It is difficult to let go of the desire to control things, to give up the need to be master of our destiny. There are too many outside forces we have no control over, but God—the infinite, almighty, omnipotent God—does. Letting go of that control requires trusting God. Oh, that is difficult! But the flip side is that we can count on God to do something good with whatever situation we are facing.

In the last chapter, we looked at God's restoring power. That is hope for the short term. We can be sure that we will not live in a state of desolation forever. In this chapter, we are going to push that hope out further and explore the long-term hope that God has for us. This hope is the one that we can really hang our hats on. If we know that we can hope in God for the long term, we have a firm foundation for life. And that is what God has promised us.

What do you hope for? What impossible dream lurks in the corners of your imagination? How would life look if everything were perfect? If you have trouble answering these questions, ask a close friend or relative to help you. What dreams do they have for you? What do they know you could do if you would only dare? Dream big. Remember, "hope that is seen is no hope at all" (Rom 8:24). In other words, think of something that is so big, only a miracle can make it happen. (If you still have difficulty, I recommend reading *The Journey of Desire* by John Eldredge.)

Now that you have an image in your mind of your dream for the future, take a step back. What does that dream rest on? Who are you going to hold responsible if that dream does not work out? Is it your parents? your spouse? your friends? your boss? Or is it God?

The only true source of hope is God. The psalmist said, "Some trust in chariots and some in horses, / but we trust in the name of the LORD our God" (Ps 20:7).

CONFIDENTLY WAITING

The prophet Micah lived during a decadent and corrupt time in Old Testament history. Both Israel and Judah were worshiping false gods, exploiting the poor and engaging in immoral behavior. Like his fellow prophets, Micah's job was to preach a clear message of grace for the repentant and doom for the disobedient. In a few short chapters he laid out his vision, and it was bleak. Still, he found reason to hope. In the last chapter of Micah, we see his confidence in the coming Messiah, in a time when God would redeem his people and restore justice and truth: "But as for me, I watch in hope for the LORD, / I wait for God my Savior; / my God will hear me" (Mic 7:7). Another translation puts it this way: "But me, I'm not giving up. / I'm sticking around to see what God will do. / I'm waiting for God to make things right. / I'm counting on God to listen to me" *(The Message)*.

Are you sticking around to see what God will do in your relationships with your parents, with your spouse, with your children? Do you have a hopeful expectation of seeing him make things right, of having him hear your prayers? This isn't some dry exercise of faith. There is a joyful anticipation in Micah's words: "I watch in hope for the LORD."

Call me a romantic, but the image that pops into my head is of a nineteenth-century sailor's wife. Even today, homes in coastal towns often feature a widow's walk, a platform on the roof surrounded by a railing. From the rooftop, a wife expecting her husband's return from sea could get a better view of the ships entering the harbor. Having watched faithfully for his ship to return, she finally spots the familiar outline of it nearing the shore, a little dirtier and more ragged than when it set out and sitting low in the water with the weight of precious cargo in its hold. The sailor's anxious wife tries to keep herself busy, knowing that it takes time to bring the ship in and unload the men and cargo. Finally, when she can wait no longer, she smoothes her hair, pinches her cheeks to put some color in them, removes her flour-dusted apron and hurries out to the front of the house. She stands there with her hand shielding her eyes from the sun, scanning the road, waiting to catch the first glimpse of her beloved as he climbs the hill from the docks and heads home. She has watched in hope, and now the day she has waited for is here.

Like that imaginary sailor's wife, we can eagerly anticipate the Lord's blessing in our lives. We can hurry out to meet him, sure that he will be there. When our knowledge of his love is firm and unshakable, we will hardly be able to contain our joy at what he has in store.

The second part of Micah 7:7 is the hardest—at least it is for me: "I wait for God my Savior." I don't like waiting. Is there a line? Forget it—I can go somewhere else or come back later. Two weeks' delivery time? You're kidding, right? Even red lights become good opportunities to read a paragraph or two in the book I'm carrying around or quickly scan the e-mail my PDA just received.

Too often I approach God with the same impatience. I want to rush God's plans. He has all of eternity, but my time is limited; can't he just hurry things up? This often becomes a checkpoint for me. If I am in a rush, it usually signals that my hope is not truly in God but in someone else or in some circumstance in my life. If my hope is fully and completely in God, then I can wait patiently, knowing that his plan is the absolute best and that he will accomplish it in his perfect timing.

THE ROAD TO HOPE

In his letter to the Romans, Paul charts the pathway to hope. Sounds great, doesn't it? A treasure map with a fantastic prize at the end. Treasure maps always sound exciting in theory—adventure, gold, swashbuckling glory, a life of ease on a Caribbean island with Johnny Depp at my side. Where do I sign up? Of course, if we actually read a couple of pirate stories, like Robert Louis Stevenson's, we learn that the reality is different. It might mean being kidnapped by dirty, foul-mouthed pirates, forced to be a galley slave, shot at by cannons, betrayed, mutinied, shipwrecked, marooned. After all that, the treasure had better live up to its hype!

Paul's treasure map to hope is not much better, I'm afraid. He charts our course in Romans 5:3-5: "We know that suffering produces perseverance; perseverance, character; and character, hope. And hope does not disappoint us." Got that? Suffering leads to perseverance; perseverance leads to character; and character—finally, mercifully—leads to hope.

As children of divorce, we've had more than our fair share of suffering. Sometimes people suffer the consequences of their own bad choices, but our suffering was undeserved. We did not do anything to bring it on ourselves, and there is nothing we could have done to stop it. So is it meaningless, worthless, wasted? It does not have to be. Remember the road map—suffering produces perseverance. If anyone has perseverance, it is the child of divorce. We have learned to adapt to new situations, to roll with the punches, to keep our chin up when we would rather just give up. That is what perseverance is: the ability to stick with it, especially when things are tough and it would be easier to throw in the towel. Our suffering has produced that in us.

And perseverance produces character. Because this book is not meant to prove anything statistical about children of divorce, or to establish new information about us as a group, I was free to interview people I knew. Most of the people I talked with were either friends of mine or friends of friends. These were not random strangers who could only reveal to me what they chose to during the hour or so that we talked about their parents' divorce. No, these were people whose lives I see day in and day out. I know their friends, their spouses, their kids, their coworkers. And what I see in each of them, without exception, is character. These are people who know the value of relationship, who know the necessity of truth, who care deeply for others and who reach out to those in need around them.

I think many of these things are evident in their lives because of the suffering they have experienced, which produced perseverance in them, which produced character. They are surrounded by the fallout of broken relationships. They have experienced firsthand the damaging effects of lies and deception. They have known deep personal pain, as well as the healing touch of a caring friend. They have persevered through their own times of sorrow and grief, and they have emerged as men and women of deep character.

Finally, character produces hope. How else can we explain the fact that so many children of divorce are actually committed to the concept of marriage? We should be the first ones to roll our cynical eyes, erect emotional barriers and live solitary lives of bitterness and anger. Instead, Brooke Lea Foster notes, "As a generation, we've embraced marriage more than our parents did. In the late 1990s, demographer Pamela Paul noticed an interesting trend. Unlike our mothers, who dreamed of careers and independence, Generation Xers dreamed of domesticity. Forget Murphy Brown. We wanted to be Donna Reed. In a 1999 poll by a national market research firm, 57 percent of Gen Xers said they 'would like to see a return to more traditional standards of marriage.'"[5] Jennifer Roback Morse, writing on Townhall.com, observed, "The younger generation is sick of the divorce culture."[6]

This is more than the wide-eyed innocence of youth. Those of us in Gen X are delaying marriage; we are not so wide-eyed and youthful anymore. So what is it? What makes us think that we can succeed where our parents failed? I think it is the hope produced by character. We know marriage takes work, and those of us who are married are committed to doing whatever it takes to make our marriages work, even if it is uncomfortable or unfamiliar. We know divorce hurts children, and those of us who have children are committed to ensuring that our children grow up with two parents who are married to each other. Those of us who are single, like me, know that there are worse things in life than being unmarried, and we have the perseverance and character to wait until we have met the right one, not just any one. Because of these things, we have tremendous hope that we will get married, that we will build strong marriages, that we will be loving and wise parents.

The character we have developed by persevering through suffering has given us a firm basis for hope. This is not a false, pie-in-the-sky, "hope that works out for you," pat on the back kind of hope. This is real hope, especially when it is hope based on a knowledge of God's faithfulness and his ability and desire to carry us through whatever we face.

And this hope does not disappoint us. Hope that is founded on God's character, on an understanding of the awesome and loving God who created us and watches over us, is a hope that will not disappoint. We will never find a time when God is not right beside us, guiding us, protecting us, making us into the people he wants us to be.

It is important to note, however, that God's treasure map to hope is one we can either follow or ignore. Not everyone who finds a yellowed, tattered map with an X to mark the spot rounds up a boatload of eye-patch-wearing cronies and sets out for mysterious islands to search for buried treasure. In the same way, not everyone who suffers perseveres. Some give up, abandon ship, decide the suffering is too difficult. They check out of life, blame their problems on others, and stay hopelessly mired in the muck of disillusionment and self-pity. The choice is ours. Will we take the path through suffering to perseverance? Will we dare to follow the treasure map to hope?

GOD'S HOPE FOR US

Standing in front of the Lincoln Memorial in Washington, D.C., in August of 1963, pastor and activist Martin Luther King Jr. intoned, "I have a dream." Those famous words and the speech that followed inspired a generation. They were words of hope and promise, words designed to challenge and motivate. The struggles of that generation are now in the history books, and a new generation has taken its place, one marked by the segregation of families, children bussed between the homes of their mothers and fathers.

To our generation (and to every generation), God has words of inspiration and hope. All through Scripture, he paints a portrait of his grace. He tells us stories in which he is the bridegroom wooing us, his radiant bride. He tells us stories in which he is our father, waiting patiently to welcome us home after we have squandered our inheritance and lost all our friends. He tells us stories in which he is our shepherd, guiding and protecting us, leading us to quiet meadows and places of rest.

The message God gives us throughout the Bible is that he has big dreams for us. He knows the chaos and tumult of our lives. Some of it we have brought on ourselves, some has been inflicted on us by those around us and some he brought to our doorstep because he knew it was what we needed, even if it was not what we wanted. He knows every dusty corner of our lives and our souls. And he has a dream for us.

In Jeremiah 29:11, God says, "I know the plans I have for you . . . plans to prosper you and not to harm you, plans to give you hope and a future." Think about that for a minute. God has dreams for your future.

Can you imagine what God's dreams for us look like? They will not be small dreams. Martin Luther King Jr., in the middle of the civil rights movement, said he dreamed of black children and white children playing together and walking hand in hand as friends. It seemed an impossible dream at the time, a dream too big, too ambitious. If a preacher in 1963 could dream such an audacious dream for a racially divided America, just think of what God must be dreaming for us!

When Jeremiah wrote those prophetic words, he was not the popular guy you might imagine. God's people had been captured by a ruthless enemy and were exiled far from their homes. The popular prophets were the ones who brashly told the people that God would overthrow the enemy and send them back to their homeland in a very short time. That was the message the people wanted to hear. Freedom and vengeance sounded good, but they were a false hope, not rooted in reality. Jeremiah's message from God was very different. He told the people they would stay in captivity for a long time, that they should get used to their situation, settle in, plant crops, try to make a normal life right where they were. The outward circumstances were not going to change anytime in the near future. But in the midst of their captivity, in the middle of their difficult situation, God wanted them to know that he still had a hope and a future planned for them.

Our circumstances are not going to change. We cannot go back to the way everything was before our parents divorced, back to living as a whole family. The myth of the "good divorce" is no better than the false hope peddled by the more popular prophets of Jeremiah's day. The divorce changed our reality, but that does not mean that we are without hope. Like the people Jeremiah prophesied to, God has hopes for us and a future planned for us. Could that future include a great marriage that lasts till death do us part? Maybe children who will learn what good parenting and a healthy marriage look like from our example. Perhaps it includes churches that become places of healing and wholeness for the broken we welcome into our midst.

Matthew Henry wrote of these words in Jeremiah, "We are sometimes ready to fear that God's designs are all against us; but as to his own people, even that which seems evil, is for good. He will give them, not the expectations of their fears, or the expectations of their fancies, but the expectations of their faith; the end he has promised, which will be the best for them."[7]

God's dreams are far better than our fears, but they are also far better than our imaginings. Paul wrote of this in his letter to the believers in ancient Ephesus: "Now to him who is able to do immeasurably more than all we ask or imagine" (Eph 3:20). Paul's description of the God he knew so well was of one who could far outpace our wildest, best dreams.

Of course, being God, he knows exactly how our future will turn out. So his dreams are not wishful thinking; they are the joyful anticipation of one who knows what is coming and cannot wait to see it happen. His dreams for us are the dreams of a father who falls asleep on Christmas Eve thinking about the joy on his children's faces the next morning when they run down the stairs and see the new bike, the smiling baby doll, the rocking horse. He knows what is in every box, what lies beneath every carefully wrapped box and perfectly tied bow. While the children lie in bed dreaming of the unknown piles of presents, their father drifts off to sleep dreaming of everything he has planned, every gift he has purchased, hidden away for a special day and put under the tree for his children to find at just the right time.

What happens to all those gifts on Christmas morning, however, depends partly on the children. Will they bound out of bed and run excitedly down the stairs to see what gifts lie in store for them? Or will they stay in bed, bored by the whole thing or sure that nothing but coal will fill their stockings? I don't know about you, but I want to tear into the presents! I want to see the abundant and abundantly good gifts that God has planned for me.

God has high hopes for us. Just as hope does not disappoint us, we do not want to disappoint hope. Someone who dreams big dreams for our future deserves to be taken seriously. So go ahead—rip open the wrapping paper!

OUR TREASURE

Just as Paul charted a treasure map for the believers in first-century Rome, we have charted our own treasure map here. In chapters one and two, we suffered through the grief of losing our families and of finding our parents to be untrustworthy or faithless. In chapters three through five, we persevered in learning that God helps us, loves us and protects us in all circumstances. In chapter six, we developed the character to see beyond the immediacy of our present suffering and perseverance to the restoration that God will begin to build from the ruins of our broken families. And in this chapter, we have followed the treasure map to where X marks the spot—to our hope.

The path and the treasure are both found in God. Paul, writing to his young protégé Timothy, began his letter by describing Jesus as "our hope" (1 Tim 1:1). The hymn writer Isaac Watts wrote, "O God, our help in ages past, our hope for years to come." God himself is our hope. He is the source of our hope, the guarantee of our hope and the fulfillment of our hope. Indeed, could we hope for anything better than to have Christ, to know him?

The New Testament book of Hebrews connects the imagery and ritual of the Old Testament to the person of Jesus Christ. The pastor or teacher who wrote this book sketched out for his readers the high priestly role of Christ and his atoning sacrifice, assuring Jewish believers that their forebears in the Old Testament were saved by their faith in the promises of God that were later fulfilled in Christ. He wanted his flock to know that the entire history of redemption, the whole story of Scripture, was centered in the person of Jesus Christ. The writer of Hebrews encouraged his readers to make their hope sure by being diligent in both faith and patience (Heb 6:11). When we persevere in this way, "we who have fled to take hold of the hope offered to us may be greatly encouraged. We have this hope as an anchor for the soul, firm and secure" (Heb 6:18-19).

Like those early Christians, we can have the hope of God anchoring our souls, firmly and securely. Some of us have spent years adrift, lost at sea after the shipwreck of our parents' divorce. We have been valiantly trying to swim ashore on our own, but we keep getting dragged down by rough waves of anger and swept away by rip currents of grief, or we crash into reefs of fear and frustration. When we stop trying to fight the ocean on our own and let ourselves be anchored in Christ, we can "be greatly encouraged."

My hope is that our journey through Scripture and through the character of God has given you an anchor for your soul. These are not principles that we can learn once and be done with. Our parents' divorce ended their marriage, but it began a new reality for us. As the years go by, new challenges and struggles will come our way, and we will need to run back to the strong tower of God's Word again and again for assurance and peace. He'll be there waiting for us.

8

Free at Last

When I was growing up, my mom never had a dishwasher. Or rather, my mom never had an *automatic* dishwasher. As my cousins and I liked to say, kids in our family were cheap labor. Mom may have been chief cook and bottle washer, but we kids were the dish dryers. Mom, who could always put her hands in water much hotter than any of the rest of us could stand, would wash the dishes, and I would dry them and put them away. During this nightly ritual, we would pass the time by either singing or talking together. To this day, certain songs conjure up images for me of a sinkful of soapy dishes.

After I left home and the job of dish drying was relegated to my younger brothers, Mom began to long for a dishwasher. The boys were not big singers. One of them refused to sing—ever— while he was in kindergarten. The boys were not big talkers either. Mom used to ask me how school was, and she'd get a litany of what happened on the playground, who got sick after lunch, when our next field trip was scheduled. The same question posed to my brothers elicited two responses of "Boring." A follow-up question of "Well, what happened at school today?" received a chorus of "Nothing." The boys preferred to pass the dish-drying time bickering, slapping each other with wet towels and negotiating with Mom over how many more dishes they each had to dry—definitely not singing or talking. Maybe it was just a clever way to get out of chores, because even today when I go home for a visit, I will linger in the kitchen to help Mom while the men retreat to the living room. And we still enjoy talking over the dishes.

So it was that sometime in my early twenties, I was standing in my mom's kitchen, dishtowel in hand, telling my mom about the spiritual truth I had been wrestling with that week. I don't remember now what prompted the realization in me, but I remember the conversation. This was during the eight years that my dad did not speak to me, and of course I had no idea then that his silence would not be permanent. All I knew was that I was tremendously hurt and even angry at Dad for cutting me off without explanation. But I had also realized something about my relationship with my dad: I had to forgive him. Not that I could forgive him, or that I should forgive him, but that I had to forgive him. That was what I was telling Mom that day in the kitchen. I knew God had forgiven me for everything I had ever done and everything I would ever do. I told my mom, "To turn around, then, and not forgive Dad for this one thing would be a slap in God's face. And it breaks my heart, because right now I just can't forgive him. I know I need to, but I can't do it right now."

THE HYPOCRITE AND THE KING

My struggle with forgiveness had very real spiritual implications. We tend to take forgiveness rather lightly, at least when it comes to whether or not we forgive others. We like to think that we can forgive if we choose, if the other person is worthy, if it suits our own personal growth. God paints a very different picture of forgiveness in his Word.

Jesus loved to teach people through parables, stories that brought the principles of godly living into the context of their own daily lives, into scenarios they could relate to and learn from more easily than didactic teaching. In Matthew 18:21-35, Jesus' story was prompted by a question from the disciple Peter: "Lord, how many times shall I forgive my brother when he sins against me? Up to seven times?" (Mt 18:21).

Now, to Peter's credit, this was a serious question and showed a generosity of spirit on his part. The other religious teachers of the day instructed their disciples to forgive three times.[1] Three is a nice, round, biblical number, and really how many of us actually manage to forgive someone for the same thing three times running? I suspect we are more inclined to say, "Three strikes and you're out." Peter realized by this point that Jesus was demolishing the pretentious, made-up rules that the religious elite had imposed on people while at the same time holding everyone to a higher moral standard than was being taught by most preachers of the day. Forgiveness falls clearly into the realm of morality, so Peter figured Jesus would demand more forgiveness than the norm. Peter took the going standard and doubled it, then added one for good measure. "How about seven times, Lord? Will that do the trick?"

The answer Jesus gave was not what Peter had hoped: "I tell you, not seven times, but seventy-seven times" (Mt 18:22). Peter was not even close. Jesus followed up his astonishing reply with a story that ought to make us all more sober about the way we approach forgiveness.

Once upon a time, Jesus told Peter, there was a man who owed a large amount of money to the king of the land. The king decided to call in his debts, but the man was unable to pay the king back. As a consequence, the king ordered that the man and his family be put in prison and all of their possessions sold. Upon hearing his sentence, the man fell at the king's feet and begged for mercy and the time to pay back the debt he owed. The king was so moved by the man's plea that he not only let him go, he canceled the man's debt altogether!

If the story ended there, we could nod in approval at the king's magnanimity and carry on with our lives. But Jesus continued the story.

After leaving the king's palace, this same man met a fellow servant who owed him a trifling amount of money. Instead of imitating the generous example of the king, the man greedily demanded that his friend pay him back immediately. When the friend asked for a little time, the man refused and had his friend jailed. He did not get away with his stinginess, however. Some other servants saw what happened and reported back to the king. "Do you remember that man who begged for mercy and whose debt you canceled? He just had another guy thrown in prison for not paying him back just a fraction of what the scoundrel owed you."

Again, if Jesus had just ended the story here, we could denounce the man as a lousy fellow and go on our way. But Jesus was not finished yet.

Once the king heard that his generosity had fallen on a hard heart, he called the man back and chastised him. "You wicked servant . . . I canceled all that debt of yours because you begged me to. Shouldn't you have had mercy on your fellow servant just as I had on you?" (Mt 18:32-33). Then Jesus tells the frightful ending to the story. "In anger his master turned him over to the jailers to be tortured, until he should pay back all he owed. This is how my heavenly Father will treat each of you unless you forgive your brother from your heart" (vv. 34-35).

Depending on your theology, these last verses can appear to mean that refusing to forgive another person means putting yourself in danger of losing salvation. But Jesus is teaching about forgiveness here, not salvation. His point is not that we can cause God to withdraw his offer of grace; his point is that God wants us to take forgiveness very seriously.

If we are followers of Christ who have repented of our sins and have been forgiven of all our past and future wrongs, we are the first servant in the story, the man who was released by the king from the vast sum we owed. When we refuse to forgive others, we are every bit as petty and ridiculous as that wicked servant who, having just been cleared of a gigantic debt, demanded payment of a few dollars from his friend.

AS CHRIST HAS FORGIVEN

We know how deeply we have been wronged. In chapter one, we considered God's intimate knowledge of our pain. We saw that God does not shy away from our hurts, nor does he ask us to pretend they do not exist. Quite often our problem with forgiveness, however, is not that we are minimizing our pain but that we are minimizing our guilt.

When I stood in my mom's kitchen and told her that I had been forgiven of every wrong I had ever done and every wrong I would ever do, that was absolutely correct. But I fear that I seldom realize just how vast my wrongdoing is. Instead I tend to think of all the wrongs I have not done. I've never done drugs, never murdered anyone, I don't cheat on my taxes. I sound like a pretty good person! Until, *ahem,* I get put under God's microscope. I secretly hated someone, cursed that slow driver in front of me, complained I had nothing to wear while standing in front of a closet full of clothes. These seem like minor things to me, but they are anything but minor to God. Just take a look at what happened to the Israelites when they complained about the food God gave them (Num 21:4-9)! It's enough to make me rethink the way I approach my closet.

God is not grading my guilt on a curve. He does not look down and say, "Well, Kristine is no Jack the Ripper, so that has to count for something." Instead, he measures my guilt against the standard of righteousness, the standard of holiness, that Jesus fulfilled. Against that standard, I am hopelessly, woefully guilty. When I see my sin in this light, the light that God views it, suddenly a whole new picture appears. Suddenly I am truly the servant who has been forgiven a debt too vast to ever be repaid.

Paul, in his letter to the Colossians, urges the church there to "bear with each other and forgive whatever grievances you may have against one another. Forgive as the Lord forgave you" (Col 3:13). This exhortation invites us to wonder how exactly the Lord has forgiven us.

First, God has forgiven us completely. We are not partially forgiven. He did not wipe out all our lesser sins and hold on to a few really bad ones that he could drag out and remind us of when he is mad at us. He cleaned the slate. In Isaiah 1:18 the Lord says, "Come now, let us reason together. . . . / Though your sins are like scarlet, / they shall be as white as snow; / though they are red as crimson, / they shall be like wool."

Have you ever tried to turn something from red to white? It is not an easy task. Just a few weeks ago as I went for a run, I somehow managed to get a cut on my toe. I felt a prick but kept going. It wasn't until I got home and pulled off my sneakers and socks that I realized the tiny cut had been bleeding and the entire toe of my sock was bright red. Not wanting to lose a pair of good running socks, I tried to get the stain out before it set. I followed Martha Stewart's instructions for getting out a blood stain. I rinsed it, dabbed it with vinegar, then sprayed it with Zout. The stain was still there. Finally I put the sock in the sink with some Woolite and let it sit for a couple hours until the stain faded to a pale yellow, only noticeable if you're looking for it.

My stain removal did the job for the most part, but God says that he takes the penetrating stain of our sins and washes them until they are as white as new-fallen snow. He does not look at us and see a faint, lingering spot of yellow. He sees the purest, brightest white, completely unsullied, as though a stain had never touched us. He forgives us completely.

In addition to forgiving us completely, God forgave us before we even asked for it. Romans 5:8 says, "God demonstrates his own love for us in this: While we were still sinners, Christ died for us." God did not wait for us to clean up our act or prove our trustworthiness. No, Jesus died for us while we were still sinners. We did not deserve this forgiveness, and we certainly did not earn it. In fact, we were reconciled to God when we were still his enemies (Rom 5:10). That does not sound like a description of people who deserve mercy.

This is where we so often fall short in our doling out of Christlike forgiveness. We have been taught to think that we do not need to forgive someone who has not asked for our forgiveness. We have been taught that others need to earn our forgiveness, to prove themselves worthy. But that is not how we have been forgiven by God. He made the way for peace when we were his enemies.

It is important to note that God requires us to forgive, but he does not require us to be foolish. (In fact, he expects us not to be foolish.) If your brother has a bad habit of stealing things, forgive him as many times as it takes—but don't leave him alone with your wallet! For one thing, it is not fair to your brother to tempt him in an area where he is known to be weak. For another, God does not ask you to be naive.

Trish's parents divorced when she was five. For years Trish did not have any contact with her dad, but eventually he began calling her occasionally to set up a lunch together or go for coffee. While Trish was glad to have the chance to get to know her father, she disliked that he came around only occasionally. Even more, she felt badly that he still would not reach out to his other children, Trish's siblings.

Things with her father continued much the same until Trish was married and pregnant with her first child. The idea of being a grandfather seemed to trigger a paternal response in her dad. Suddenly Trish's father wanted to have a bigger role in her life.

Knowing the pain that her dad's lack of presence had caused in her own life, Trish was determined to protect her children from experiencing the same fickleness from their grandpa. Trish sat her dad down and told him there were some ground rules if he wanted to be a part of his grandchild's life. Most importantly, he had to commit to being consistently involved, not just showing up when he felt like it and then disappearing again for months.

Trish wonders hopefully about the impact all of this has had on her dad, seeing the daughter he abandoned twenty-five years ago showing him grace and forgiveness. As his relationship with his oldest daughter has begun to heal, Trish's dad has started building a relationship with another one of his children.

Trish welcomed her father into her life and let him know that she loved him and forgave him. But she also let him know that she had a responsibility to protect her children and that his access to them depended on him abiding by the rules she and her husband had established. Forgiving her dad did not mean that Trish had to expose her own young children to the whims of an occasional grandfather.

HOW JESUS FORGAVE

Even knowing that Jesus is God in the flesh, the forgiveness Jesus showed others is still shocking, at least to me. Think of Christ's words as he hung in agony on the cross: "Father, forgive them, for they do not know what they are doing" (Lk 23:34). To forgive people who are so clearly in the wrong when you are completely innocent—when you are the only one who can rightly be called completely innocent—requires humility. It requires a conscious laying aside of one's rights and a purposeful mindset of obedience.

We see a glimpse of this just a few hours before Jesus hung on the cross interceding for his enemies. Jesus was enjoying a meal with his disciples, and John wrote, "Having loved his own who were in the world, he now showed them the full extent of his love" (Jn 13:1). No, he did not pass out party bags with gifts tailored to each one's interests—a new fishing pole for Peter, matching "sons of thunder" T-shirts for James and John. Instead, Jesus wrapped himself in a towel and proceeded to wash his disciples' feet.

Foot washing sounds odd to us, but it was an important gesture of hospitality in a culture where one's feet were the primary mode of transportation. That also meant it was a smelly, dirty job. Feet that spent long hours on dusty or muddy roads were bound to be sweaty and smelly. The lowliest servant usually got this least desirable assignment.

This was not Jesus' job, nor was it a quaint and familiar ritual between teacher and students. It shocked the disciples. Their teacher, their Lord, should not have been washing their feet. Peter, never afraid to speak up, insisted that he would not let Jesus wash his feet. It was undignified and backward. But Jesus told him, "Unless I wash you, you have no part with me" (Jn 13:8), so Peter relented.

This story is familiar to many Christians. We know that Jesus washed his disciples' feet. Some churches even host foot-washing ceremonies, especially at Maundy Thursday services before Easter. But what we may be overlooking is the reason Jesus was able to humble himself in this way.

John explains that the meal was already underway. He tells us Satan had already tempted Judas to betray Jesus. Then he gives us a pivotal point: "Jesus knew that the Father had put all things under his power, and that he had come from God and was returning to God" (Jn 13:3).

Jesus could confidently walk through life, taking the abuse of the Pharisees and then the physical abuse of a torturous death, humbling himself daily, even washing the dirty feet of his followers, because he knew where he had come from and where he was going.

Imagine how our lives would be different if we had that same confidence. Where did we come from? Well, we are made in the image of God (Gen 1:26), we are God's children (1 Jn 3:1), we are the handiwork of God (Eph 2:10). What better place to be from, than the hand of God!

Years ago my grandmother started tracing our family's lineage. What began as a hobby blossomed into a treasure trove of stories, pictures and genealogical charts filling dozens of three-ring binders. After listening to her talk about it so much, I too caught the bug and began to dig deeper into our past. While researching an ancestor who had come to America in the 1600s, I found a family tree someone else had compiled. It showed that our ancestors could be traced back through European history all the way to Charlemagne, the first emperor of the Holy Roman Empire and progenitor of all the royal families in Europe from the Middle Ages on. The discovery made me feel somewhat regal, and I began to sign my name with more care—after all, I was the descendant of kings and queens. Royal blood flowed through my veins. As God's dearly loved children (Eph 5:1), we can all sign our names with a royal flourish. We are sons and daughters of the King of kings!

And where are we going? We are destined for heaven. In the Bible's hall of faith, Hebrews 11, we read of the Old Testament saints:

> All these people were still living by faith when they died. They did not receive the things promised; they only saw them and welcomed them from a distance. And they admitted that they were aliens and strangers on earth. People who say such things show that they are looking for a country of their own. If they had been thinking of the country they had left, they would have had opportunity to return. Instead, they were

longing for a better country—a heavenly one. Therefore God is not ashamed to be called their God, for he has prepared a city for them. (Heb 11:13-16)

Jesus said much the same thing to his disciples: "In my Father's house are many rooms; if it were not so, I would have told you. I am going there to prepare a place for you. And if I go and prepare a place for you, I will come back and take you to be with me that you also may be where I am" (Jn 14:2-3).

We have come from the hand of God, and we are headed to the place he has prepared for us. When we begin to view life from that macro level, suddenly the disagreements we have and the injustices we suffer seem small by comparison. What is a rude word when compared to heaven? All the hurt and pain that our parents have brought into our lives pale in comparison to eternity.

PRACTICAL STEPS

In spite of the theological necessity to forgive, we often find ourselves unable to forgive on a personal level. That is where I found my-self that day in my mother's kitchen—perfectly aware of my need to forgive, and perfectly aware that I did not have it in me at that moment to forgive on my own. So how do we get over that hurdle and find a way to forgive?

The first step is to understand the theology of forgiveness. We have unpacked some of it here, but Scripture is one long tale of forgiveness and reconciliation, so we have barely scratched the surface of what God has to say on this subject. To go deeper, you could sit down for a few hours (or days or weeks) with a concordance or a good topical index of the Bible and trace the path of forgiveness from Genesis to Revelation.

The second step is a little more painful. It involves repentance. Unfortunately, our definition of repentance has become pretty watered down. Whenever a celebrity makes a misstep, we hear a quick mea culpa and then learn which rehab center will provide public atonement. Too often, though, this display is meant to blame an addiction for whatever wild behavior or politically incorrect speech landed the celeb in hot water. Repentance, by contrast, is about accepting blame—not shifting it. It involves a true mea culpa, an acknowledgment that I am the guilty one—in this case, guilty of holding on to resentment and an unforgiving spirit. Repentance also involves a commitment to change, a turning away from the confessed behavior or attitude and a turning toward a new way of living and thinking.

Third, we need to consciously let go of our resentment and our perceived right to be angry over the hurts inflicted on us. Paul wrote to the church at Philippi, "Your attitude should be the same as that of Christ Jesus: Who, being in very nature God, did not consider equality with God something to be grasped, but made himself nothing" (Phil 2:5-7). Jesus provided a model of humility for us, but humility goes against our human nature. Paul once boasted of his claims to be a good Jew (2 Cor 11:21-28). He was trying to make a point, but his right to boast pales in comparison to the rights of Jesus: Son of God, sinless, creator of the universe. Jesus' bragging rights were bona fide, but he humbled himself for our sake and set the ultimate example of humility. We may feel that we have every right to be angry and hurt, and we may be right. But humility calls us to lay aside even our legitimate rights for the sake of something better, something higher.

There is one more thing we need to let go of, and that brings us to step four. We need to let go of our expectations. More specifically, we need to let go of the notion that we can achieve some kind of picture-perfect relationship with our parents. When our parents hurt us, it can be tempting to think that if we can just reconcile, everything will go back to the way it was before. It is a nice fantasy, but it is probably unrealistic and therefore can be damaging to the process of forgiveness. When our dream of having everything the way it used to be crumbles or fails to materialize, we can be hurt all over again and begin to doubt whether this forgiveness stuff is worth it.

This is not to say we should be cynical, expecting nothing but a lifetime of hurt from our parents. Just because the relationship will never be exactly what it was before does not mean we can't forge a new relationship that is stronger and better than the one broken by careless words or thoughtless actions. It is the same in our relationship with God. We will never go back to the sinless state of humanity in the Garden of Eden, but in its place we have the compassionate grace and forgiveness of our Lord, a tender expression of his love that is in some ways sweeter than the original because it is offered in spite of our abject failure.

There is no magical step five, I'm afraid. In the end, forgiveness is a choice. It is something we choose to do, in spite of the real harm the other person has caused us, in spite of their not deserving forgiveness, in spite of the fact that we cannot reclaim the relationship we once had. Steps one through four can help us get to the place where we make that choice, but we must finally make the choice either to forgive or to hold on to our hurts.

Sometimes we try to complicate things. If the answers are complicated, then our inability to apply them is not our fault. We are off the hook. We can wallow in sin, self-pity, unforgiveness, selfishness, whatever. We are like the Pharisee who heard Jesus say that if he loved God and loved his neighbor, he would be fulfilling all of the law and commandments—but then asked, "Who is my neighbor?" (Lk 10:29). The Pharisee wanted to complicate things, to make up a schematic for who qualified as his neighbor and who did not, to figure out whom he was obligated to love and whom he could pass by.

When the answers are simple, though, we are stripped of our excuses. We are accountable for applying the things we know. Love, forgive, hope, trust. These are not difficult concepts. The difficulty is in applying them, in being obedient to what we know we should do.

Forgiveness is an act of stunning selflessness. It runs counter to every instinct we have to protect ourselves, and it is a supremely risky undertaking. There is no guarantee that the person being offered forgiveness will accept it. There is no guarantee that they will treat it as the precious gift it is. They may be like the ungrateful servant in Jesus' parable, shoving our forgiveness carelessly in their pocket and walking away without their heart being changed. They may turn around and hurt us another seventy-six times. In light of these realities, it seems more prudent to put limits and conditions on our offer of forgiveness. "I forgive you" ought to be followed by forty-five seconds of fast-talking car-commercial disclaimers.

Alexander Pope was writing of literary criticism when he penned the words, "To err is human, to forgive divine," but his sentiment is true. Erring is in our very nature as humans. From the moment that Eve bit into the forbidden fruit and passed it over to her willing husband, the human race has been careening toward error, toward sin. We hurt each other, we offend God, we ruin ourselves. It is what we do and who we are. There is no use denying it or trying to get around it. We are absolutely and completely sinful. By contrast, God's very nature includes forgiveness (and, of course, so many more things). Eve's fruit picnic was no surprise to God. He knew exactly what she and Adam would do when tempted. Long before God created Adam from dust and Eve from a spare rib, God had a plan to redeem his people, to offer us forgiveness and reconciliation. Everything he does, even his justice and retribution, fits into his grand scheme for redemption.

Forgiveness truly is divine. When we forgive others who have wronged us, when we take such an enormous risk with another errant human, we follow in the very footsteps of God. He took a risk with us. Will we find it in our hearts to take the same risk with those who have wronged us?

9

Getting Past "Our Father"

When I was six years old, I sat on a plastic chair in the basement of a church in Decatur, Illinois, and watched and listened as one of our junior church leaders read a missionary story to us. I loved the flipbook missionary stories, with their simple drawings of faraway places and the children and adults who learned about God and began to follow him, often at great peril. This one was about a boy in the Philippines, I think, whose grandfather was a witch doctor. When the missionary came to their village and told them about God, the little boy believed, but his grandfather threatened to kill him for his new faith. Eventually the grandfather and most of the rest of the villagers followed Jesus, and the little boy was safe from harm.

Somewhere in the middle of this story was a clear explanation of the gospel—that we are sinners who have disobeyed God, that God sent his Son to die for our sins, that we needed to be sorry for our sins and ask God to forgive us and save us. It was a simple gospel, but it was enough for a six-year-old mind to grasp. When the junior church leader asked if anyone wanted Jesus to be their Savior, I raised my hand. A few minutes later, I kneeled with one of the helpers on the concrete floor behind an accordion door, confessed my sin and asked God to come into my life.

I may have been young, but my commitment to Christ was real. Like most new believers, I eagerly read my Bible and enthusiastically witnessed to everyone I knew, telling them the good news about Jesus. As I grew older, I remained steadfast in my faith, and my mom and stepdad sent me to Christian schools where my understanding of God and his role in the world was nurtured. Just as I reached an age where my teen spirit wanted to rebel, my parents put me in public school. Suddenly my rebellion, my desire to be different, could take the form of being a Christian. I even got called into the principal's office once for inviting kids to Campus Life and carrying around a Bible, and I defiantly told her that what I was doing was perfectly legal and she could not stop me. If she wanted to try to stop me, I insisted that there were plenty of law firms that would be only too happy to take my case pro bono (not knowing a single one, of course, but certain they abounded). My blustery defiance worked, and the principal backed down.

My only real crisis of faith came when I was in my twenties, sinking into depression after a breakup with a boyfriend. In my sadness, I began to question everything I had always known about God. I quickly discovered that my faith was too deeply rooted for me to even begin to question God's existence. To imagine that God did not exist was rather like imagining that I did not exist, a notion so absurd that I could not even begin to take my mind there. Rather, my journey was like the one C. S. Lewis described after the death of his wife, Joy. He was not afraid so much that he would stop believing in God, but he wrote, "The real danger is of coming to believe such dreadful things about Him. The conclusion I dread is not, 'So there's no God after all,' but, 'So this is what God's really like. Deceive yourself no longer.'"[1]

During that dark time in my life, I wrestled with God, trying to discover what he was really like. Was he a God of love, who cared about me and was involved in my life? Or did the deists have it right when they described God as a cosmic watchmaker who set the world in motion and then sat back to observe it disinterestedly?

Many of the things I have written in this book about God's character are things I learned—not just heard or was taught, but really learned—during those months of wrestling. Like Jacob, who wrestled all night with an angel of the Lord and would not give up until he was blessed (Gen 32:22-32), I persevered through the depths of depression and spiritual numbness until God blessed me with an assurance of his character and his love.

I tell you this because this chapter is probably the hardest one for me to write. This chapter is about the barriers to faith that children of divorce experience, and the truth is that I have been only peripherally challenged by these barriers. I am a little like the rich man trying to write a thesis on poverty after spending a month in the ghetto. These issues are not the ones that have caused me to question God, and even my questioning of God has been from a wholly faith-filled perspective. Still, I know from my reading and from the people with whom I have talked that there are real barriers to faith for children of divorce, barriers that arise directly from our family situations. Some of those barriers are erected by the failures of our parents, and sadly, many are erected by the failures of the church.

FATHER GOD

In *Between Two Worlds*, Elizabeth Marquardt explores the inner lives of children of divorce, including spirituality. In the study that formed the basis for her book, she found that children of divorce are less likely to embrace faith. However, she found that those who do embrace faith are more likely to be evangelicals.[2] One of the reasons for this, Marquardt concluded, is the "father language" they use to talk about God.

Using father language to talk about God is a barrier to faith for many children of divorce. We hear that God is our father, and instinctively we think of words like abandonment, loss and unfaithfulness. Those of us who have seen our fathers leave our family, who have seen our fathers have affairs with other women, who have been the child afraid that daddy no longer has time for us, can think that a God who is called Father will be the same way. Who is to say that God will stick around, that he will love us always, that he will never forsake us? If he is our father, well, we know what to expect from that kind of relationship, and it is not good.

Of course, God is not like our human fathers, but we so often get things all turned around. We begin to judge God based on what we see in those around us. In a sense, we begin to make God in our image when it is the other way around. God is not made in our image. He is not subject to our fallibility and our fickleness. Instead, we are made in his image, which can present a problem of its own. If we look in the moral mirror, what we see is not so pretty. Mirror, mirror, on the wall, who's the most sinful of us all? The answer is always, "You are!" Perhaps if we are made in God's image, God is not so hot. At least we can be tempted to think so when we look at his supposed reflection in our own lives and in the lives of those around us, especially those who have let us down.

But the image of God in us was broken, damaged back in Eden when Adam and Eve bit into the fruit and introduced sin into our world. We no longer reflect God's image the way we should. The Bible tells us over and over to be holy, to be pure, to love each other, while simultaneously acknowledging that there is no good in us, that our good works are nothing but filthy rags. We are made in God's image, but we are very poor representations of that image. In our best moments, we give off a faint glimmer of the perfect love and holiness that is God.

On the other hand, the father language that the church uses to talk about God can also be what draws us to faith. Marquardt's finding that most of us who find faith are evangelicals is, she says, because of two factors. One reason is that evangelical churches have been more welcoming to divorced families; but the second reason is that evangelical churches tend to use more father language for God.

While some of us are unwilling to approach a God who might be like our fathers, others are eager to embrace a God who is the Father we never had. If we accept as true the picture of God that Scripture gives, then here we have a Father who is everything we have always wanted in a father, lived out perfectly. He is all the things we find lacking in our earthly relationships but now find that we can have with our heavenly Father. For those who approach God in this way, his role as our Father is a great comfort, a relief and joy.

WE WELCOME EVERYONE—SORT OF

While the church, and particularly the evangelical movement, uses father language for God that can be a welcome mat for those who need a better image of a father, the church can also be a barrier to faith for children of divorce. When Paul's parents divorced, he lost more than his family. Looking back, he sees that the church he grew up in had an unhealthy dynamic, but at the time it was his family's faith community, the place where they experienced and learned about God. That changed, though, when his parents' marriage began to dissolve. When the divorce finally happened, Paul's mom was cut off from their church amid false rumors and innuendo, and she was shunned by many of her former friends. Her children felt condemned by their church as well. The people who should have been their spiritual family cut them off and turned them away.

Sadly, the church has done a poor job of dealing with the reality of widespread divorce in our society over the last thirty years. Too often the church has maintained a strict silence on the topic, either out of fear that mentioning it could spread the contagion or out of an unwillingness to pronounce judgment anywhere. Neither response is correct, and both responses have left children of divorce feeling like outsiders in a community that should be the place they can call home.

For ten years my family attended a church where we were not members. In fact, we were not allowed to be members. We were excluded from membership because my mother was divorced and remarried. Never mind that her divorce had taken place years earlier, never mind that her first husband was not a believer and that he was an adulterer, never mind that my mom had long since repented for her role in the divorce and sought God's forgiveness. None of this mattered. We would have fared better if she were a recovering alcoholic, a cleaned-up junkie, even a reformed prostitute. Those were all forgivable sins and made for good testimonies. But she was a divorcée, a sin from which one could not recover, according to this church. This was not a place of welcome and redemption. It was a place where we were never good enough. There was no repenting for this past sin, no making it better, no chance of ever being a full part of the body of Christ.

Unfortunately, our experience was not unique. Different churches and denominations adopt different interpretations of the biblical injunctions against divorce. While Christians may disagree on the parameters of biblically sanctioned divorce, it seems clear that we should welcome fellow sinners who have fallen on their knees before God, repenting of their former sins and experiencing his grace. We should not be creating two classes of Christians—the forgiven and the marked for life.

SO WHAT *DOES* THE BIBLE SAY?

About the time we started attending that church, I decided I did not like part of the Bible. I don't know whether I found these verses on my own or whether they were part of a Sunday school lesson or sermon, but I took issue with Jesus' teaching in Matthew 5 that a woman divorced for any reason other than adultery becomes an adulteress. Channeling my inner Thomas Jefferson, I simply took a black pen and inked out the offending words. I was probably eleven or twelve at the time and had not yet learned of my father's infidelity, nor had I been in a church that taught anything more about divorce than a passing "don't do it."

My parents were never ones to believe in the right of privacy for their children. They paid for the space we called our bedrooms, so they figured they had a right to go in and look around occasionally. My modified Bible was soon found, and I heard a stern lecture on Revelation 22:18-19 about not adding to or subtracting from God's Word. My parents wanted me to know that I could not simply ignore the parts of the Bible I did not like. If I did not like it, I needed to study it more to see if maybe I was understanding it incorrectly, or I needed to study myself to see if I was simply feeling guilty about not keeping part of God's law.

At some point I did learn the circumstances of my mom and dad's divorce, and I wrestled with the various interpretations given by pastors and churches through the years that either condemned or exonerated my mother as a divorced and remarried woman. One camp thought there was no justification for remarriage after a divorce. Although they did not come right out and say it, this rendered my mother's marriage to my stepfather invalid—hardly a comfort, especially when I considered that it made my two brothers illegitimate. Another camp thought that remarriage was okay because my father was an unbeliever and an adulterer. They said that according to the original Greek Scripture, it was as if such a man were dead, which was good news for my mom but kind of awkward for me. Did that make me a half-orphan, and did that mean I could not go visit him anymore? Should I call my summer visits with Dad séances since I was visiting the dead? I knew the answer to those questions was no, but it did highlight the flawed reasoning of that teaching, at least from the perspective of the child.

Making things worse, none of this teaching came from the pulpit. Sure, if you scheduled an appointment with the pastor, he would be happy to sit down and discuss what the Bible has to say about divorce. But teaching from the pulpit on the subject of divorce was conspicuously absent.

Scripture is not silent on the subject of divorce. If it were, we would have no justification for pronouncing judgment. There are a number of key Bible passages on the subject of divorce (see appendix B). I will leave it to the scholars and seminarians to debate the proper interpretation of these and other passages on divorce. My intention is not to settle these debates, as if that were possible, but simply to urge the church to provide solid teaching on this subject.

In 1 Corinthians 7, Paul answers questions about marriage asked by the church in Corinth. Was it better not to be married at all? Did that mean they should divorce their current spouses? Since they should not be married to unbelievers, did that mean they should divorce their unbelieving spouses? What about widows? Were they allowed to remarry? And if so, to whom? Corinth was a sophisticated metropolis, and the church there was dealing with a whole host of messy situations: incest, divorce, lawsuits, dietary rules, chaotic church services—the list goes on. These were more than hypothetical questions for the Corinthians. They had real issues for which they needed real guidance, and Paul was patient enough to address each one in turn.

In the same way, the church today faces issues that are more than just hypothetical, including questions of divorce. One-third of

Christians who marry will divorce.[3] When we add in the children of those dissolved unions, it is not a stretch to think that more than half of the adults sitting in church pews on any given Sunday are either divorced or have divorced parents. That is not even counting all the others who have been touched by divorce in some way because a relative or close friend has experienced a divorce. Perhaps more than any generation since Paul's day, divorce is an issue that affects today's church, and pastors and church leaders need to understand the issue and be willing to patiently address it, like Paul did.

THE OTHER SIDE

If one segment of the church is too quick to condemn and exclude families in which a divorce has taken place, another segment is perhaps too welcoming. There is a fine line between a "come as you are" mentality and an "anything goes" standard of behavior.

The "anything goes" philosophy sounds good when we are the sinner receiving abundant grace over and over again. Such cheap grace, as Dietrich Bonhoeffer termed it, is shallow and detrimental to spiritual growth, but it feels good to be able to do whatever we want under the cover of forgiveness. Paul anticipated such a response when he taught about the magnificent grace of God in his letter to the Romans: "What shall we say, then? Shall we go on sinning so that grace may increase? By no means!" (Rom 6:1-2).

Churches should be places of grace, but sometimes they become places where grace is used to excuse sin. Pastors may even encourage divorce for people in unhappy marriages. That's what happened in the family of Rob Evans. Evans has his own line of Christian CDs and videos for kids, setting Bible stories to music as the Donut Man. He appears in churches all over the United States and Canada, singing his songs and teaching children about God. There was a time, though, when Evans was not a churchgoer. In an interview with *National Catholic Register,* Evans said, "When my parents divorced when I was 6, the church in Paoli (Penn.) told [my mother] that divorce might be the best thing for her in this situation because she found 'true love' with another man and that she had her whole life ahead of her. The church did not fight for the unity of our family. . . . So we stopped going to church."[4]

Churches that take a lax view of divorce—allowing it for trivial reasons or even encouraging individuals to seek divorce outside of biblical parameters—not only corrupt grace, they hurt the children of divorce. They cheapen marriage, making it disposable, and in the process tell the children of divorce that what happened was perfectly fine and normal and sometimes just happens when grownups cannot get along. This is a wholly unsatisfying answer to a child, teenager or adult whose family has just been ripped in two.

When the church fails to hold us to a higher standard—whether in business dealings, sexuality, marriage or any other facet of life— we lose what makes the church distinctive. God tells us again and again in Scripture that we are set apart and holy, and that we are to live holy lives. We need the help of the church in this quest. We need pastors and church leaders who will call us to be holy and who will let us know when our lives are meandering outside the boundaries of holiness. We need shepherds who are willing to tend the flock and keep us in the fold, not letting us wander aimlessly around the mountainside peering over cliffs and into lions' dens.

Addressing the sin in our lives is an acknowledgment of our brokenness. We are fundamentally broken before God. Our relationship with him has been severed by sin, and only his grace can restore it. Any child of divorce will tell you about the brokenness of a family torn apart. We even use the term "broken home" to talk about divorce. We do not come from "a home where things just did not work out" or "a home different from other people's homes." We come from broken homes. Sweeping divorce under the rug of grace and embracing everyone without telling them about God's requirement of holiness minimizes the brokenness that children of divorce feel when they look at their families.

WHAT'S A CHILD OF DIVORCE TO DO?

All of this "father language" that the church uses can sound either comforting or revolting, depending on our point of view. And then there is the church itself, full of imperfect, sinful people, just like us, who sometimes make a mess of following God and leave a trail of broken hearts in their path. Is it all just hopeless? Should we give up on God and decide that faith is impossible? Of course, my answer is a resounding no. If the answer is no, then how can we get past these real barriers to faith?

Many of the books for parents and counselors that are aimed at helping us children of divorce warn that we are apt to blame ourselves for our parents' split. If we were young at the time, we may have felt that we could have prevented the divorce if we had been better behaved or less trouble. If we had already left home when our parents split, we can feel guilty that we were not there to smooth things over, that our leaving home somehow caused the whole thing to crumble. What none of those books talk about is our tendency to blame God.

Many of us blame God for our parents' divorce, and it is understandable. Surely God could have stopped our parents from getting a divorce. If he is sovereign, isn't the whole thing his fault anyway? If it is his fault somehow, then we are justified in turning our backs on him, in being angry at him and refusing to step foot in his house. God thus becomes our scapegoat (Lev 16:7-22). We can tie the scarlet thread of our parents' divorce around his neck and send him stumbling off into the wilderness, never to be seen again. On the other hand, we might do well to remember that the scapegoat was guiltless, qualifying it to bear the sins of others. God bears no guilt for our sins. We are wholly responsible for them. He bears no guilt for our parents' divorce. They made their own choices, rightly or wrongly, and any guilt is theirs and theirs alone.

The bigger issue that I think most of us struggle with is judging God for the failures of the church. When Christians let us down, we can feel that God has let us down. The church is the body of Christ. When we feel slapped around or overlooked by the church, we can begin to feel that God has done the slapping and ignoring.

This certainly is not an issue limited to the children of divorce. People have used the failures of the church as a reason to stay distant from God for generations. To hear people talk about the Inquisition, the Salem witch trials and the Crusades, one would think these were all current events instead of centuries-old failures on the part of the church. We hear that the church is full of judgmental people, hypocrites and intellectual lightweights. And it is true. There are a lot of broken, messy, unlovely people in the church, people who gossip and complain and generally make themselves and those around them miserable.

Our mistake, though, is in making God guilty by association. "If that's who he calls his people, I want nothing to do with him," some say, instead of realizing that it must take an extraordinarily patient and loving God to put up with all of our nonsense.

God is not defined by how well we live out his principles. He is defined by himself: holy, loving, protecting, all-knowing, all-powerful, faithful and compassionate. He is all these things and so much more. My dad's third wife once marveled that she had friends who studied theology in school. "All four years of college, they studied God," she said to me, obviously wondering how it could possibly take that long. "It's a lifetime of study," I told her.

Even a lifetime is inadequate to plumb the depths of God's nature. He is compassionate, faithful and loving, our source of help and strength, the one who restores us and gives us hope.

Having such a God, we can confidently say what the apostle
Paul said:

> We are hard pressed on every side, but not crushed; perplexed,
> but not in despair; persecuted, but not abandoned; struck
> down, but not destroyed. . . . Therefore we do not lose heart.
> Though outwardly we are wasting away, yet inwardly we are
> being renewed day by day. For our light and momentary trou-
> bles are achieving for us an eternal glory that far outweighs
> them all. So we fix our eyes not on what is seen, but on what
> is unseen. For what is seen is temporary, but what is unseen
> is eternal. (2 Cor 4:8-9, 16-18)

THE COMFORT YOU HAVE RECEIVED

In chapter one, we looked at the comfort we have received from
God. We said that God expects us to pass that comfort on to others. Paul called God "the God of all comfort, who comforts us in
all our troubles, so that we can comfort those in any trouble with
the comfort we ourselves have received from God" (2 Cor 1:3-4).
All around us there are families falling apart, couples teetering on
the brink of divorce, children whose hearts are breaking because
Mom and Dad no longer live together.

I never thought much about other children who were dealing
with their parents' divorce until I was asked to help lead the
Sunday school class for young children at my church. While I
cannot pretend that we solved the problems those young children were dealing with, I do know that they appreciated having a place in the church where people knew about the terrible
thing happening to their family, a place where they could talk
about their fear and anger and anxiety. All of us leading the
class were ourselves the children of divorce. We had once been
in their shoes, but without the benefit of a place in the church to

talk about the things that weighed on our hearts.

My hope and prayer is that, as we have journeyed together through the pages of this book, you have experienced the hope and healing that comes from knowing the depth of God's love for you. That is not my only hope, however. I pray that all of us would become advocates and intercessors for other families in trouble. I pray that we would stand firmly on the side of marriage, encourage others to honor and cherish their spouses, and live our own lives in ways that uphold biblical standards. I pray that, on behalf of other children of divorce who may not have a voice, we would speak out about the heartache we have experienced and the incredible hope and healing we have found in Christ. I pray that we would find ways to reach out to the families in our own churches and communities that have been touched by divorce. When we do these things, we redeem the tragedy of divorce that struck our family, turning it into something that brings hope to others and glory to God.

Appendix A

A Note to Parents

My guess is that some of the people who will pick up this book are not themselves children of divorce. Some readers are parents who are going through a divorce, contemplating a divorce or who have already divorced. Others may be the grandparents, aunts and uncles, spouses or close friends of someone who is a child of divorce.

First, let me say that you are an honored guest on this journey of discovering God's love for children of divorce. Without the tender care of our parents, grandparents, extended family and other loved ones, this journey would be so much more difficult. Thank you for caring enough about us to pick up this book and learn about this pivotal experience in our lives.

Let me also congratulate you on making it this far—assuming you have not skipped right to this chapter! Some of the things you read in this book may have been painful for you to read. Some are painful because they reveal to you, perhaps for the first time, the depth and breadth of the pain that accompanies having one's parents divorce. As someone who loves us, it hurts you to know that we endured such things. Some things are painful because they expose ways that those around us contributed to our wounds.

I imagine this book has not been easy for you to read, but hopefully you have gained insight into not just our sorrow but also into the ways that God brings hope and healing to our lives. I hope this book has helped you see how you can be an encouragement and source of comfort to the child of divorce in your life.

If you are a parent considering divorce, I hope with all my heart that you will do whatever you possibly can to save your marriage. Except in cases where there is physical violence or extreme conflict, studies show that children do better in unhappy homes than in split homes.[1] If you have learned nothing else from reading this book, you should know by now the devastating consequences of divorce on your children. Yes, God can heal their hearts, but how much better if you do not bring that kind of pain into their lives.

If you picked up this book hoping to find justification for your decision to leave your marriage, hoping to learn that somehow your children will be okay in the long run, I am afraid this is not the book for you. The truth is, if you are unhappy in your marriage, you need to weigh your unhappiness against your child's well-being. Because I have never been married, I cannot begin to imagine the depth of loneliness and heartache that attend an unhappy marriage. But I have tried to give you a glimpse here of the loneliness and heartache that attend being a child of divorce.

You would not be reading this book if you did not love your children, so I can only hope that you will choose your love for them over your own temporary happiness. Those words likely sound harsh and impossible if you are in a desperately unhappy situation. One study found, however, that two-thirds of couples who were unhappy but remained married found new happiness in their marriage within five years.[2] In other words, if you give it some time, your marriage may get better.

Fighting for your marriage will not be easy, and you may not succeed. If you do not succeed, at least give yourself and your children the satisfaction of knowing that you tried every possible way for as long as you possibly could. While we would love to see our parents stay together until death do them part, we at least want to know that they did not cavalierly discard their marriage and the bond that held us together as a family. We want to at least know that you tried your best to make it work and only abandoned ship as a very last resort.

You may be going through a divorce or have already been through one, through no choice or desire of your own. In these days of "no fault" divorce, there is often little you can do if your spouse chooses to leave the marriage. No one has to prove that the other spouse was guilty of anything to dissolve the bonds of marriage. Even a marriage that began with Christ at its center can fall apart if one spouse turns their back on him or willfully pursues sin.

If that is the situation you find yourself in, please do not beat yourself up over the pain that your children have experienced. We were there, and we understand that you were a victim of divorce just as we were. This book is about hope—the hope that is found in Jesus Christ. Make sure that your children know who God is and that they have an opportunity to experience him deeply. Talk about God with them often, and let them see what a difference he makes in your life. If you can show your children how God has healed your own broken heart, you will help them see how they can have the same hope.

It reassures us when you let us know how God has given you strength and healing after a painful divorce. No matter how close we have been, how many fights we have had, how many times we have hurt each other, we still love you. You are, after all, our parent, a bond that transcends the everyday ways that we get on each other's nerves. We care deeply about you, and when we see you hurting, we hurt as well. Many times we have not told you about the pain that divorce has caused us because we wanted to protect you. We knew you were hurting and we did not want to make it worse by adding to your burden. When you talk to your adult children about how God is working in your life to bring you healing and new life after divorce, you help us to know that you are in his hands and that we can release our burden of worrying for you.

IT'S NEVER TOO LATE

Perhaps you are the parent who walked out on your marriage, for another person or for personal fulfillment or for something else. Maybe you have made so many mistakes with your children that you wonder if the damage can ever be repaired.

The good news is that as long as you and your children are still living, it is never too late to begin to mend that broken relationship. After eight years of silence from my dad, and more than thirty-four years after he and my mom divorced, Dad and I are rebuilding a relationship. There is no quick fix for a relationship that resembles little more than a pile of rubble. Land must be cleared, the rubble sorted through to find what still works and what must be discarded, foundations marked and laid, then brick piled on brick in a painstaking process before anything of substance will begin to emerge.

Twelve years after my dad's silence was broken, I have been delighted by his encouragement. I carry around on my PDA an undeleted e-mail message from him congratulating me on an article I wrote, calling it "insightful and moving," and signed "Love, Dad." When I left my longtime job at a nonprofit organization earlier this year to write and do consulting work, Dad sent me a long e-mail titled "Bravo!" In it he offered advice from his own experience of building a movie production company, a business based on networking and freelancing. These words of encouragement from him are like words of life spoken into our relationship.

No matter how bad things get, no matter how many mistakes have been made on both sides, we love our parents. Even as we acknowledge their flaws, we hope for the best, and we hope for something beautiful to emerge from the rubble.

I recently talked with a friend who is a child of divorce and has a fractured relationship with her mother. There have been deep gashes of pain between this mother and daughter, wounds that are still visible on my friend's face as she talks about the things she experienced growing up. You might think that she would walk away, wash her hands of a mother who not only inflicted this pain but still refuses to acknowledge it. Instead, she told me of her failed attempt to see her mom on Mother's Day and how sad she was that her mother had declined to see her. The day we honor our mothers would seem to be the last day this wounded daughter would want to celebrate, yet she longs for healing in her relationship with her mother. Nothing can change the past, but she knows that the future could be so different if only her mother would try to bridge the distance.

If you have found yourself estranged from your child and wondering if things can ever be made right, the answer is yes! Take the first step and reach out to your son or daughter. Invite him to have a cup of coffee with you. Send her flowers on her birthday. Begin to clear the land of rubble, and soon you will be building a new future together.

MORE WORDS OF LIFE

Many of the lists of dos and don'ts for divorced parents include "Don't talk negatively about your former spouse." There is good reason for this. While divorce may sever the bonds of marriage, it does not sever the bonds of a parent and child. Biologically, half of our DNA comes from that other parent. When you criticize our other parent, we feel the sting ourselves. We fear that, along with our freckles and the ability to curl our tongue, we might have inherited the dishonesty or slovenliness or whatever it is you comment on each time our other parent's name comes up in conversation.

Few divorces are without acrimony, and frankly if you are such good friends with your former spouse that you have nothing bad to say about him or her, perhaps the marriage should have continued. More likely though, you have a long list of grievances and some very good reasons for being angry and upset with your former spouse. You will do yourself and your children a world of good if you bite your tongue whenever there is even a chance that your children will hear your words.

Mimicking Jesus' style, I would like to raise the bar: You have heard it said, "Don't speak negatively about your former spouse," but I tell you, say good things about your former spouse whenever possible, especially when your children are around. Affirm to your child that there was a reason why you married their father or mother in the first place. Affirm that there are very good things that your child has inherited from their other parent.

My mom and I agree that my dad is a charming person. He has an easy manner, an intelligent mind and a quick wit, all of which combine to make him a person that people want to be around. I inherited my sense of humor from Dad, as well as an interest in photography. Recently my stepfather was admiring some photographs I had taken and hung in my living room. "These are really good," he said, glasses perched atop his head so he could study them better. "You really inherited an eye for photography from your dad." These small affirmations of good things in me that come from my dad are more words of life to my soul. They are especially life-giving coming from my mother and stepfather.

My dad's parents regularly asked about my mom and stepfather and brothers. They wanted to see pictures of the two little boys who were no relation to them but were so important in my life. My grandpa once said of my stepfather, "Ken has been a good dad to you all these years, hasn't he?" It was a statement, not a question, and I agreed with him. It was a comfort to him to know that I was being taken care of, and it was a comfort to me that he would affirm this important relationship in my life.

Often we children of divorce feel like we have to keep our families separate. When we are with one parent, we feel that we should not talk about the other parent. We know there is animosity there, we know it is awkward and in some cases we know there are consequences for talking about the things that happen at our other parent's house. So we learn to compartmentalize, to sift our memories and our words, only letting those fall through that pertain to the family we are currently with. When our families talk about each other in positive ways, it is a relief for us to know that we do not have to be so careful to parse our lives.

So rather than simply refraining from speaking ill of your ex-wife or ex-husband in front of your kids, try to see if you can find ways to speak positively of him or her. It may be a difficult challenge, but if you can rise to it, you will breathe life into your child and into his or her relationship with your former spouse.

MAINTAINING CONTROL

No matter when a divorce occurs, one thing is certain: the children involved will feel like their world is spinning wildly out of control. Everything that has been sure and steady in their life is suddenly shaken up. Mom and Dad no longer live together. Siblings may be split apart. The family home may be sold. Schools may change. The family finances may be radically different.

I interviewed children of divorce who had experienced the breakup of their families at all different stages of life, and they confirmed that there is no such thing as a good time in a child's life for a divorce to occur. One man whose parents divorced when he was a young boy said it was like a death that never stopped.

Another whose parents divorced when he was a teen said divorce may be the worst tragedy that can befall a child. Yet another, who was already out of college when his parents' marriage fell apart, described the event as his own personal 9/11.

Even though most of us know that statistically we are far more likely to die in a car accident than in a plane crash, many people feel more nervous about flying than about driving to Grandma's for Thanksgiving.[3] Why would we ignore the facts? Why does flying scare us more than driving, even though it is safer? The answer is that we are not in control when we are forty thousand feet in the air, encased in a metal fuselage, hurtling toward our destination. If the plane begins to go down, all we can do is grip our armrests, review the emergency instructions we ignored before takeoff and pray. By contrast, we feel like we are in control when we are behind the wheel of our own car. If something goes wrong, we can slam on the brakes or take evasive action. We can do something to control our environment. Our circumstances have not really changed, and in fact we are in more danger; but we feel better because we have some control over the situation.

As a parent, you can give your children the same sense of control when their world is being shaken apart by divorce. You may not be able to stop the divorce or change the past, but you can help restore some calm to your children's lives by carving out areas where they can have control.

One of my friends is a former teacher and now a stay-at-home mom to two little girls. When one of her daughters was on medication that made her feel hungry all the time, my friend made up a picture chart of acceptable snacks and hung it on the refrigerator. Instead of having to constantly tell her three-year-old daughter no because she was asking for ice cream or whatever food sounded good to her abnormally hungry belly at the moment, my friend created a situation where she could say yes to her daughter's choice of foods from the refrigerator chart. Cheese sticks, grapes, strawberries, a glass of milk, pretzels—the little eating machine could have whatever she wanted, all day long, as long as it was on the chart. Mom's solution preserved her own sanity while giving her child a feeling of control over an unusual situation.

How you implement this will depend entirely on your family situation and your child's ability to make wise choices. Your child's life has been turned upside down, and many things are out of his or her control. Things will never be the way they were before the divorce, and a lot of things will change immediately and for the long term.

My mom and stepdad were brave. Although I was only four years old when they met and five when they married, they actually came to me and asked my permission to marry. They explained that this decision would affect my life every bit as much as it affected theirs, and they wanted me to have a part in the decision. This was a wise choice, and it helped us all mesh as a family right from the start—but it was incredibly brave! I guess they knew me well. I remember thinking that I had to say yes, because they wanted to get married, and I wanted them—my mom particularly—to be happy. I had a sense of the power I held in this situation, and also a sense of the responsibility to do the right thing.

After they got married, my mom let me decide what I wanted to call my stepfather and whether or not I would be adopted by him. I chose to call him by his first name and to not be adopted. That was important to me. To do otherwise somehow felt like a betrayal to my dad, who would always be my dad no matter what happened. The important thing, though, is not what I chose but the fact that I had a choice. These were small decisions in the big scheme of things. My mom made it very clear that my stepfather would love for me to call him Dad and to legally adopt me. I was assured of his love, and at the same time I was allowed to make a choice that honored my feelings.

If your children are no longer young, give them the freedom to make decisions about where to spend vacations and holidays. Some of the adult children of divorce I know have whirlwind holiday celebrations, popping in and out of mom's and dad's and the in-laws' houses like whack-a-mole arcade games. A new comedy film, scheduled to be released for the upcoming holiday season, is titled *Four Christmases*. It tells the story of a married couple who each have divorced parents. But for many children of divorce, the holidays are no joke. Most of them keep up their elaborate juggling routine not because they want to but because they know they will suffer the consequences if they do not. Mom will cry, dad will sulk, everyone will make them feel guilty for not showing up. So instead they have progressive dinners: appetizers at dad's, dinner at mom's, dessert at the in-laws'.

Things are only further complicated when children of divorce have children of their own. People I interviewed told of having to carefully coordinate their parents' visits to the hospital when grandchildren were born lest Grandma and Grandpa run into each other and create a scene. They told me about having to plan separate parties to celebrate their children's birthdays and graduations because Grandma and Grandpa cannot get along.

If you are the parent of an adult child of divorce, give him or her some sense of control by showing you can be trusted to not cause a scene in front of your grandchildren. Let your child have the freedom to decide to spend a holiday away from you or a vacation without visiting you. Like the mother who put the snack chart on her refrigerator for her preschooler, you will find that you will reap the benefit of giving your grown child this freedom of control. Instead of being a two-hour stop in the whirlwind holiday tour, you can enjoy longer periods of uninterrupted time with your adult child. But the real benefit is the unstrained relationship you will have with your child when he or she feels free to make decisions without the burden of guilt or the fear of conflict.

TO TELL THE TRUTH

One of the most difficult balancing acts that parents who divorce are faced with involves what to tell their children about the divorce. On the one hand are families where the divorce is shrouded in secrecy, no one talks about it, we all go along trying to pretend that everything is fine and normal and let's please not talk about unpleasant things. At the other end of the spectrum—particularly when empty-nesters divorce—are families where nothing is sacred, where Mom and Dad feel free to talk to their kids about how unsatisfying their sex life had been or speculate about who the other party slept with before, during and after the divorce papers were filed.

Our families help us define ourselves, help us explain who we are and how we got to be this way. Whether it is the quirks and habits we have developed through the years or the physical traits we inherited, we look to our family to see where we have been and where we might go. When vast parts of our family history are off-limits, we are confined in our understanding. The copper highlights in my hair made a lot more sense when I learned that my grandpa and great-grandma had both been redheads in their youth. So in one sense, the facts about our parents' divorce can be revealing. They can help us understand crucial bits of information about our family history and about ourselves.

But on the other hand, children can be given too much information, too many intimate details about their parents' relationship. When parents share this kind of information with their children in a casual manner, it can be just as damaging as hiding everything. Brooke Lea Foster wrote, "Parents forget that just because we're in our twenties doesn't mean we feel any less like their son or daughter. Hearing details of their problems—learning how miserable they've been—tears us apart inside. We have a personal stake in the loss. It's painful to listen to."[4] This often happens when a parent does not have anyone else who can offer the emotional support the marriage once provided. In this case, it is better to find a trusted friend or a counselor who can listen and provide guidance, rather than relying on one's children.

Somewhere in the middle of these two extremes is a happy medium, and the parameters for that middle ground will change as your children age. When they are very young and ask questions about the divorce, you can answer them matter-of-factly without offering unnecessary details. As they grow into their teen years, their questions will be more sophisticated and will likely be more about the why than the what of divorce. These are key years when children are beginning to approach adulthood, and the things they learn about themselves and about the way people relate to one another will help form a foundation for their later success in life.

As your children grow into adulthood, you can begin to share more with them. Especially as your children begin to form romantic attachments and think about marriage and children of their own, they will want to understand more of the nuances of how your marriage began, what made it good, what made it difficult, what you might have done differently if you had it to do over again.

You will have many opportunities to talk with your children about your divorce as they grow and ask questions. Those questions might seem daunting because it feels like there is a right and wrong answer, but there isn't. Your children simply want to know the truth—nothing more, nothing less. If you can give them the truth, not only will you help them understand you better, you will help them understand themselves.

ALL IN THE FAMILY

After my dad's parents passed away, my uncle was sorting through some of their papers and found a box of letters. Many of the letters were ones that I sent them, but the box also included letters that my mom sent to my grandparents, beginning shortly after her divorce from my dad and continuing until I was about ten. Mom's letters recounted stories about my friends at school, funny things I had said or done and summaries of my report cards. They also recorded the back-and-forth negotiations that preceded my annual summer trips to visit Ponci and Grandpa—when I could travel, how long I could stay, would they please not shower me with too many gifts.

I was touched when I first read those letters, especially since I was reading them from an adult perspective. I wondered if I would have had the fortitude to send detailed letters to my former in-laws after a painful divorce, and for such a long time. Mom's willingness to do so was a wonderful, previously unknown, reminder of her love for me. Because she loved me, she kept in touch with my dad's family, ensuring that I had a strong relationship with them all those years.

Keeping the lines of communication open with your former spouse and your former in-laws, particularly if you have young children, is a way to show your love for your children. The rich relationships we have with our families give us more opportunities to experience love and show love, and they help shape us into vibrant adults who can in turn shower love on the next generation. Your gift of self-sacrifice for your children will build a legacy of love for years to come.

THE BEST ADVICE

Finally, pray for your children. This is the best tip I or anyone else can give you. If you are a follower of Jesus Christ, you serve a God who cares about and loves your children more than you do, as hard as that is to imagine. And you serve a God who is all-powerful and always present, one who can watch over your children perfectly at all times. Prayer is your line of communication to God, and it is the best method you have for protecting your children.

Let your children see you praying for them. My mother fondly tells of the week she got to spend at her grandma and grandpa's tiny, four-room house each summer when she was a child. Although all their grandchildren lived nearby, every summer they invited each one individually to spend a week at their house. It was their week alone with Grandma and Grandpa, and it was a special time. But what my mom most remembers about those weeks was seeing Grandma and Grandpa kneeling beside the sofa each evening, praying together to close their day. Their simple evening routine was an example to my mom of their dedication to prayer and their love for God. Like my great-grandma and great-grandpa, you can become a model for your children of a praying man or woman. In so doing, you will not only be surrounding them with God's care and protection, you will be giving them a spiritual example to follow that will protect them all their lives.

As a parent, you have been chosen by God to create life and nurture it to adulthood. In this you are God's creative partner. This is not a task for the faint-hearted. But with God's gracious help, you can guide your children so that, like the boy Jesus, they grow "in wisdom and stature, and in favor with God and men" (Lk 2:52).

Appendix B

What the Bible Says About Divorce

We tend to think of divorce as a modern invention, a product of the twentieth century. Divorce, however, has been around since the earliest days of civilization, and the Bible directly addresses the topic a number of times. Listed below are some of those passages, along with a brief summary of their content.

- Leviticus 21:7, 13-15; Ezekiel 44:22: Priests should not marry divorced women. High priests are further restricted from marrying widows or anyone who is not a virgin.

- Leviticus 22:13: The divorced daughter of a priest may return home to live if she has no children, and she may then eat the food provided to Levites as part of their inheritance.

- Numbers 30: Widowed or divorced women who make vows are bound by them. (Married women could have their vows nullified by their husbands; likewise, unmarried women could have their vows nullified by their fathers.)

- Deuteronomy 24:1-4; Jeremiah 3:1: A woman who remarries after a divorce cannot go back and marry her first husband again, whether her second marriage ends in divorce or death.

- Isaiah 50; Jeremiah 3: God divorced Israel because of its unfaithfulness.

- Malachi 2:10-16: God hates divorce.

- Matthew 1:18-25: Jesus nearly became a child of divorce. Joseph was going to quietly divorce Mary, his pregnant fiancée, until an angel intervened.

- Matthew 5:31-32; 19:1-12; Mark 10:1-12; Luke 16:18: A man who divorces a woman except for adultery makes her become an adulteress; a man who marries a divorced woman commits adultery.

- 1 Corinthians 7: Do not divorce just because you are married to an unbeliever. If the unbeliever leaves, though, let him or her go.

Acknowledgments

Special thanks are due to several key individuals who helped and sustained me through this process.

My parents, Ken and Terrie Meyer, and my dad, Bill Steakley, have always encouraged me, and I am grateful to them. They, along with the rest of my family, have graciously let me write about our lives together, both in this book and on my blog, childofdivorce-childofgod. blogspot.com. My dear friend Lori Smith has given me courage and endurance when I needed it most, in writing and in life. My friend Catherine Larson deserves my humble gratitude for introducing me to my wonderful editor, Al Hsu. Al believed in this project from the beginning and served as my guide on this first-time journey through the publishing process. My church family at Guilford Baptist prayed for me, encouraged me and held me accountable during the writing and editing process, and my pastor, Mike McKinley, ensured that I did not write anything heretical. Linda Jacobs at DivorceCare for Kids was my personal cheerleader, urging me to complete this project.

Finally, I am tremendously grateful to the other children of divorce who openly and graciously shared their stories with me. Your willingness to tell your stories has enriched this book immeasurably.

Notes

Introduction

[1] Rebecca Salois, "When Parents Divorce, Kids' Pain Can Be Lessened," *Indianapolis Star*, May 28, 2006.

[2] Vicki Lansky, *Vicki Lansky's Divorce Book for Parents*, 3rd ed. (Minnetonka, Minn.: Book Peddlers, 2005), p. 56.

[3] e. e. cummings, *Complete Poems, 1904–1962*, ed. George J. Firmage (New York: Liveright, 1991), p. 663.

[4] George MacDonald, *Discovering the Character of God* (Minneapolis: Bethany House, 1989), p. 19.

Chapter 1: The Trouble We Have Seen

[1] Pia Nordlinger, "The Anti-Divorce Revolution: The Debate on Marriage Takes a Surprising Turn," *The Weekly Standard*, March 2, 1998.

[2] Judith Wallerstein and Sandra Blakeslee, *What About the Kids?* (New York: Hyperion, 2003), p. 26.

[3] Theresa Walker, "Torn Asunder: Coping with Divorce," *The Orange County Register*, April 23, 2006.

[4] "Not-So-Happy Newlywed," December 23, 2005 <www.uexpress.com/dearabby/?uc_full_date=20051223>.

[5] Matthew Henry Concise Edition, Classic Bible Commentaries <eword.gospel com.net/comments/psalm/mhc/psalm56.htm>.

[6] Bill Hybels, *The God You're Looking For* (Nashville: Thomas Nelson, 1997), pp. 16-17.

[7] Neil Kalter, *Growing Up with Divorce* (New York: Free Press, 1990), p. 207.

[8] Zora Neale Hurston, *Their Eyes Were Watching God* (New York: Harper & Row, 1990), p. 23.

[9] Quoted in Hybels, *God You're Looking For*, p. 4.

Chapter 2: Faith(fulness) of Our Fathers

[1] Jeff Giles, "The Poet of Alienation," *Newsweek*, April 18, 1994.

[2] Jen Abbas, *Generation Ex* (Colorado Springs: WaterBrook, 2004), p. 118.

[3] John Trent, *Breaking the Cycle of Divorce* (Carol Stream, Ill.: Tyndale House,

2006), p. 15; also see Neil Kalter, *Growing Up with Divorce* (New York: Free Press, 1990), p. 11.

[4] Rob Bell, *Velvet Elvis* (Grand Rapids: Zondervan, 2005), p. 25.

[5] Spurgeon's Treasury of David, Classic Bible Commentaries <eword.gospel com.net/comments/psalm/spurgeon/psalm13.htm>.

[6] C. J. Mahaney, *Living the Cross-Centered Life* (Sisters, Ore.: Multnomah, 2006), pp. 32-33.

[7] Brooke Lea Foster, *The Way They Were* (New York: Three Rivers Press, 2006), p. 51.

[8] Mathew Henry Bible Commentary, Classic Bible Commentaries <eword .gospelcom.net/comments/psalm/mh/psalm9.htm>.

[9] Jamieson, Fausset, and Brown, Classic Bible Commentaries <eword.gospel com.net/comments/hebrews/jfb/hebrews6.htm>.

[10] Spurgeon's Treasury of David, Classic Bible Commentaries <eword.gospel com.net/comments/psalm/spurgeon/psalm9.htm>.

Chapter 3: The Weight of the World

[1] Michael J. Bradley, *Yes, Your Teen Is Crazy! Loving Your Kid Without Losing Your Mind* (Gig Harbor, Wash.: Harbor, 2002), p. 145.

[2] Judith Wallerstein and Sandra Blakeslee, *What About the Kids?* (New York: Hyperion, 2003), p. 233.

[3] Elizabeth Marquardt, *Between Two Worlds* (New York: Crown, 2005), p. 111.

[4] H. Norman Wright, *A Dad-Shaped Hole in My Heart* (Grand Rapids: Bethany House, 2005), p. 103.

Chapter 4: All You Need Is Love

[1] Greg Garber, "Jailed Tanner's Losses: Game, Set, Match . . . Family," ESPN, June 24, 2006.

[2] Leonard Kass, "The End of Courtship," *Boundless Webzine*, Focus on the Family <www.boundless.org/2005/articles/a0001158.cfm>.

[3] "Let Us Love One Another," 1 John 4:7-12, IVP New Testament Commentary, BibleGateway.com <www.biblegateway.com/resources/commentaries/index .php?action=getCommentaryText&cid=14&source=1&seq=i.69.4.3>.

[4] Bill Hybels, *The God You're Looking For* (Nashville: Thomas Nelson, 1997), p. 26.

[5] Matthew Henry Bible Commentary, Classic Bible Commentaries <eword .gospelcom.net/comments/psalm/mh/psalm139.htm>.

[6]Dawn Eden, *The Thrill of the Chaste* (Nashville: W Publishing Group, 2006), p. 39.

[7]John Gill's Exposition of the Bible, Classic Bible Commentaries <eword .gospelcom.net/comments/isaiah/gill/isaiah54.htm>.

[8]Archibald MacLeish, *J.B.* (Boston: Houghton Mifflin, 1958), p. 14.

[9]John Piper, "A Service of Sorrow, Self-Humbling, and Steady Hope in Our Savior and King, Jesus Christ," Sound of Grace <www.soundofgrace.com/ piper2/piper2001/9-16-01.htm>.

Chapter 5: Things That Go Bump in the Night

[1]Judith Wallerstein and Sandra Blakeslee, *What About the Kids?* (New York: Hyperion, 2003), p. 226.

[2]Neil Kalter, *Growing Up with Divorce* (New York: Free Press, 1990), pp. 46, 180.

[3]Elizabeth Marquardt, *Between Two Worlds* (New York: Crown, 2005), p. 34.

[4]Ibid., p. 59.

[5]Ibid., p. 20.

[6]Meg Meeker, *Strong Fathers, Strong Daughters* (Washington, D.C.: Regnery, 2006), p. 144.

[7]Marquardt, *Between Two Worlds*, pp. 60-61.

Chapter 6: All Things Made New

[1]Kevin Leman, *Making Sense of the Men in Your Life* (Nashville: Thomas Nelson, 2000), p. 78.

[2]Donald Miller, *To Own a Dragon* (Colorado Springs: NavPress, 2006), p. 43.

[3]"The Plague of the Locusts," Minnesota Historical Society Virtual Resources Database <www.stolaf.edu/depts/environmental-studies/courses/es-399%20home /es-399-02/McLeod/Grasshoppers/Grasshoppermain.html>.

[4]Laura Ingalls Wilder, *On the Banks of Plum Creek* (New York: HarperCollins, 1965), pp. 194-95.

[5]Quoted in Hampton Keathley IV, "Joel," The Minor Prophets, Bible.org <www.bible.org/page.php?page_id=968>.

[6]Ibid.

[7]Bertha Spafford Vester, excerpt from a book called *Our Jerusalem*, It Is Well with My Soul <spaffordhymn.com/html/history.html>.

[8]John Gill's Exposition of the Bible, Classic Bible Commentaries <eword .gospelcom.net/comments/ezekiel/gill/ezekiel37.htm>.

[9]Spurgeon's Treasury of David, Classic Bible Commentaries <eword.gospel

com.net/comments/psalm/spurgeon/psalm71.htm>.

Chapter 7: More Than a Statistic

[1] Jeffrey Zaslow, "Emailing the Ex: How Technology Can Help Ease Divorce Dealings," *The Wall Street Journal*, November 4, 2005.

[2] Judith Wallerstein, Julia Lewis and Sandra Blakeslee, *The Unexpected Legacy of Divorce: A 25 Year Landmark Study* (New York: Hyperion, 2000), p. 290.

[3] Ibid.

[4] Karen S. Paterson, "Man Behind the Marriage Amendment," *USA Today*, April 12, 2004.

[5] Brooke Lea Foster, *The Way They Were* (New York: Three Rivers Press, 2006), p. 251.

[6] Jennifer Roback Morse, "Holidays Without Homes," Townhall <www.townhall.com/columnists/JenniferRobackMorse/2005/12/26/holidays_without_homes>.

[7] Matthew Henry Concise Edition, Classic Bible Commentaries <eword.gospelcom.net/comments/jeremiah/mhc/jeremiah29.htm>.

Chapter 8: Free at Last

[1] John Gill's Exposition of the Bible, Classic Bible Commentaries <eword.gospelcom.net/comments/matthew/gill/matthew18.htm>.

Chapter 9: Getting Past "Our Father"

[1] C. S. Lewis, *A Grief Observed* (New York: Bantam, 1961), p. 5.

[2] Elizabeth Marquardt, *Between Two Worlds* (New York: Crown, 2005), p. 156.

[3] The Barna Group, "Born Again Christians Just As Likely to Divorce As Are Non-Christians," *The Barna Update*, September 8, 2004 <www.barna.org/FlexPage.aspx?Page=BarnaUpdate&BarnaUpdateID=170>.

[4] Tom Wehner, "He Was an Evangelical Until He Read Aquinas," *National Catholic Register*, December 24-January 6, 2006 <ncregister.com/site/article/1653/>.

Appendix A: A Note to Parents

[1] Alan Booth and Paul R. Amato, "Parental Predivorce Relations and Offspring Postdivorce Well-Being," *Journal of Marriage and the Family* 63, no. 1 (2001): 197-212.

[2] Linda J. Waite et al., *Does Divorce Make People Happy?* (New York: Institute for American Values, 2002).

[3]Jeffrey Kluger, "How Americans Are Living Dangerously," *Time*, November 26, 2006.

[4]Brooke Lea Foster, *The Way They Were* (New York: Three Rivers Press, 2006), p. 5.

About the Author

Kristine Steakley is a freelance writer and a grant-writing consultant living in northern Virginia. She is a graduate of Messiah College in Grantham, Pennsylvania, and worked for more than a decade at Prison Fellowship Ministries. She is a blogger for The Point (<www.thepoint.breakpoint.org>) and also blogs at <www.childofdivorce-childofgod.blogspot.com>.